Act

07 |6.

Sir John

Sir John

The Many Faces of Gielgud

**CARICATURES AND COMPILATION BY
CLIVE FRANCIS**

**FOREWORD BY
SIR ALEC GUINNESS**

Robson Books Ltd

First published in Great Britain in 1994 by Robson Books Ltd,
Bolsover House, 5–6 Clipstone Street, London W1P 7EB

Illustrations copyright © 1994 Clive Francis
Compilation copyright © 1994 Clive Francis
The right of Clive Francis to be identified as author of
this work has been asserted by him in accordance with the Copyright,
Designs and Patents Act 1988

British Library Cataloguing in Publication Data
A catalogue record for this title is available from the British Library

ISBN 0 86051 903 1

Designed by Linda Wade

Photoset by Rowland Phototypesetting Ltd, Bury St Edmunds, Suffolk
Printed in Great Britain by Butler and Tanner Ltd, Frome, Somerset

Acknowledgements

I'm greatly indebted to everyone who has personally contributed to this book. Their affectionate and amusing remembrances have been instrumental in making this a glorious celebration for Sir John.

My thanks also to Louise Dixon, my editor, who bravely took on the idea without seeing a single drawing, to my loyal and brilliant agent Clare Vidal-Hall, to Nina Thomas for her diligent research, and lastly to my darling wife and children for all their encouragement and support.

Clive Francis

Original Contributions

Lindsay Anderson ✳ Edward Bond ✳ Richard Briers ✳ Annette Crosbie
Constance Cummings ✳ Judi Dench ✳ Michael Denison ✳ Michael Feast
Robert Fleming ✳ Edward Fox ✳ William Fox ✳ Clive Francis
Christopher Fry ✳ Patrick Garland ✳ Dulcie Gray ✳ Alec Guinness
Peter Hall ✳ Robert Hardy ✳ Robert Harris ✳ Wendy Hiller
Anthony Hopkins ✳ Michael Hordern ✳ Glenda Jackson ✳ Bernard Levin
Robert Lindsay ✳ Anna Massey ✳ Geraldine McEwan ✳ Ralph Michael
Julian Mitchell ✳ John Moffatt ✳ John Mortimer ✳ Vanessa Redgrave
James Roose-Evans ✳ John Schlesinger ✳ Paul Scofield ✳ Donald Sinden
Maggie Smith ✳ Georg Solti ✳ Geoffrey Toone ✳ Wendy Toye
Dorothy Tutin ✳ John Warner ✳ Irene Worth

Foreword

SIR ALEC GUINNESS

*N*ot all of us will survive to celebrate John G's hundredth birthday in ten years' time but I'll bet my Equity subscription that he is as upright, debonair and brilliantly tactless then as he is now.

It is sixty years since I first worked for him, in his definitive Hamlet of 1934, and although he has lost none of his authority and charm in the intervening years it is impossible to convey to a younger generation the glamour and theatrical innovations he represented. He has straddled the English theatre for most of this century as the exemplary actor, his head thrown back as if peering beyond us, his eye clear as an April morning, his voice always instantly recognizable and thrilling. In younger days an exotic whiff of Cypriot cigarettes preceded him as he entered the stage door, his smart black trilby hat tilted over his nose; and his manner was a rather unsettling combination of courtesy, exasperation and professional impatience, as if nothing must impede his progress to his dressing-room and the stage. He was hero-worshipped by many young actors like myself who copied, in the cheapest form possible, his outward trappings without being able to emulate the inner man.

I think it must have been the first time I lunched with him and two or three of his cronies that I was deeply shocked at the way they sent him up – although it was something he seemed to quite enjoy. At the time he was speculating about what he might do next – a revival of a Chekhov, a new version of *A Tale of Two Cities*, a Shakespeare comedy – I can't remember now all the chopping and changing of his innumerable schemes. In the midst of his rapid chat one of his friends suddenly said, 'Oh, shut up, dear! Just stick a crown on your head and get on with it.' Which, of course, is exactly what he did. It was a rare year that passed without him wielding a sceptre; and his generosity was always equally royal. Books, neckties, cuff-links and dinners came the way of all of us; and, on one occasion, the loan to my wife and me of his pretty cottage at Finchingfield in Essex for our honeymoon.

Some of us, revering him and loving him as we did, had to pay a sort of emotional Danegeld to his directorial frustrations. One mid-morning (happily, I was not in the play) he sacked the entire cast of a comedy he was producing. 'You're fired! You're fired!' he shouted at every actor who spoke a line. Finally Fay Compton, who was a great star of the period, intervened to say, 'John, are you all right? You appear to have lost your head.' 'And you're fired, too!' he rapped out. Ten minutes later everyone was reinstated and it was hugs, tears and kisses all round.

In the early thirties John lived in a small flat over a saddlery shop in St Martin's Lane, very convenient for the New Theatre (now the Albery) where he had so many triumphs and within two minutes' walk of the Motleys' studio, where most of his productions were endlessly discussed and finally designed. Now he lives in a Stately Pleasure Dome (built, I would like to think, of ten thousand dropped bricks) in a remote part of Buckinghamshire, surrounded by dogs, birds and beautiful things. One of his bricks, a golden one, was dropped many years ago at a luncheon he was giving to the playwright, the late Edward Knoblock. John remarked of someone, 'He's as boring as Eddie Knoblock. Oh, not *you* Eddie. Another Eddie Knoblock.' The timing of course was impeccable.

Although he appears to be happy I think he is impatient with life unless there is immediate work on hand. *The Times* crossword, which he does in a few minutes flat, is not enough; he needs a dozen scripts piled up to pick and choose from, to discuss with friends and to change his mind about a dozen times a day.

Introduction
CLIVE FRANCIS

The stage-door keeper stared hard and long, blew his nose and ran a nicotine-stained finger down a long list of names.

'Been 'ere before?' he said, roughly crossing mine out in red biro.

'Yes,' I replied.

'Well, you'll know your way around then, won't you,' and jerked his head towards the pass-door.

The year was 1967 and, to my astonishment, I had been recalled to The Queens Theatre to meet John Gielgud, who was about to direct Peter Ustinov's *Half-way Up the Tree* for Binkie Beaumont.

I was greeted warmly by the stage manager and ushered to the side of the stage where a script, which I had now become quite familiar with, was gently slipped under my arm.

'Mr Clive Francis, Sir John.'

The announcement was made and on I walked, stumbling into the glare of a brightly lit stage, nervous at the prospect of meeting the man I most admired in the theatre.

There then followed a penetrating silence, followed by a loud rustling of papers and a lot of coughing. The tall lean figure of Sir John could vaguely be seen disentangling itself from an aisle seat. Swiftly he moved towards the stage, a cigarette stylishly hanging from his lips, and began to stare up at me in bewilderment.

'Oh God, no. No, no, no, no. I'm more than certain I didn't ask for you back again.'

Luckily my career did not finish there on that wet September afternoon – though at the time I do remember thinking how convenient it would be if the stage just opened up momentarily so I could step neatly into hell, and have done with it.

Apart from a brief moment in Sheridan's *The Critic* for the BBC, in which Sir John was cast, wonderfully and extravagantly, as Lord Burleigh, a non-speaking cameo turn – can you imagine it, the most mellifluous voice in the English-speaking theatre, and not a single syllable was heard. Except, as I remember, a cough!

Apart from that, it was sixteen years before our paths crossed again.

The setting was Jaipur, Rajasthan, in India. The film was M M Kaye's *The Far Pavilions*. JG was Sir Louis Cavagnari and I was his faithful doctor, Rosey.

Being an epic drama you found yourself sitting around mercilessly for hours on end, while hundreds of startled extras were repeatedly put through their paces. A painfully slow process as one was up against interpreters not always interpreting the right instructions or, in some cases, needing an interpreter to assist the interpreter – as the interpreter didn't, or wouldn't, speak English.

But the waiting was never tedious when Sir John was sitting with you. Always warm and amusing, he would enthusiastically while away the time with fantastic talk and glorious stories, which just poured out of him at an effortless speed.

One day the maharajah and his family arrived to watch filming and nestled themselves along the front of the battlements as if it were the dress circle of the Theatre Royal, Haymarket. It was a scene where the palace was being stormed by marauding Afghan rebels, and Gielgud, brandishing a pistol, tried to quell the revolt with a long and heroic speech.

During all of this, the royal family sat silently sipping cups of tea and nibbling Madeira cake. They were so overcome that the great Sir Gielgud was gracing their presence, that when he finished his speech they all rose to their feet and applauded. Sir John, slightly taken aback by this impromptu ovation, smiled and charmingly nodded to each in turn.

It was then discovered that there was a hair in the gate (a flaw on the film) so that the speech had to be repeated all over again; and then repeated rather a lot. And each time the maharajah, now feeling honour bound, responded with the same enthusiasm, until it became faintly irritating.

One day JG and I took a taxi to the Amber Palace, a beautifully preserved historic monument perched high on the edge of a steep hill. The only way to reach the top was either by foot or the gentle hump of a camel.

'Strange looking beasts, aren't they, camels,' he said eyeing one rather warily. 'Edith Evans once said I reminded her of one.' And began, without hesitation, to climb the steep path. He was eighty-one at the time.

There have been so many wonderful stories about him and his various gaffes – or bricks, as he likes to call them – many of which I'm sure are apocryphal. Like the time, for instance, he was at a Hollywood party surrounded by a number of keen admirers. On being asked whether he was enjoying his stay in Los Angeles he replied that he was, apart from some of the film personalities whom he found rather tedious.

'I was cornered at dinner the other evening by that insufferable George Axlerod. Do any of you know him?'

There was a slight uneasy shuffle.

'Well, Sir John . . . I'm, er . . . I'm George Axlerod.'

'Really!' beamed JG, 'what a coincidence.'

I have admired John Gielgud all my life. In fact ever since I bought my first record at the tender age of ten, the Shakespearean anthology *The Ages of Man*. I can remember being captivated by the lyricism and perfection of his phrasing, the power and beauty of his voice – 'never has English sounded more beautiful from the human mouth' – and at the way the text was made so simple and clear to understand.

There have been volumes of words written about him, and as many witty stories told, that I'm not going to try and compete in any way with what has gone before. More to the point I couldn't – I'm not a writer.

What I have tried to do in this book is create a pictorial essay of one man's brilliant and dazzling career, through the all-winking, all-seeing, eye of caricature. Not, I hope, in a critical or displeasing way – although naturally that opinion can only rest in the eye of the beholder – but with sincere affection and respect.

Ever since he was sixteen, when he made his Shakespearean debut as Orlando in an amateur production of *As You Like It* – fiercely drawing his sword and declaiming, 'Forbear, and eat no more,' but then, unfortunately, tripping over a large log and falling flat on his face – John Gielgud has enjoyed one of the longest and most distinguished careers in theatre history. His influence on the British stage since his glorious successes of the 1930s at The Queen's is immense and immeasurable.

It is in recognition of all that is now, and all that has gone before, that we salute him. We wish him great and future happiness.

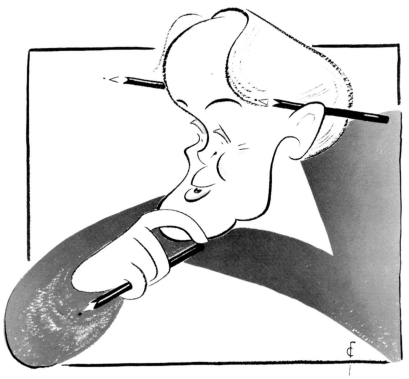

When your great-aunt happens
to be Ellen Terry; your great-uncle
Fred Terry; your cousins
Gordon Craig and Phyllis Neilson-Terry
and your paternal grandmother
Aniela Aszpergerowa, Lithuania's greatest
Shakespearean actress – you're hardly
likely to drift into the fish trade.

CLIVE FRANCIS

SYBIL THORNDIKE

One class I had [at RADA], it must have been about 1922, was really awful – they were all like a lot of governesses, no power, and I said, 'You're all terrible, no fire, no guts, you've none of you got anything in you except that boy over there, the tall one, what's your name?' And he said, 'It's John Gielgud,' and I said. 'Well, you're the only one.' The rest of them had no voices, and I was furious with the principal because all his pupils were perfect ladies and gentlemen and that's no way to do Greek tragedy. They all looked as though they were training to be Gerald du Maurier.

JOHN GIELGUD

At sixteen: I affected very light grey flannels braced much too high, silk socks, broad-brimmed black soft hats, and even, I blush to admit, an eye-glass upon occasion. And I wore my hair very long and washed it a great deal to make it look fluffy and romantic.

A few days after Gielgud arrived
at his first drama school,
Lady Benson (the principal)
burst out laughing in the
middle of a rehearsal and
pointed at him in dismay:
'Good heavens, you walk
exactly like a cat with rickets!'

I wore white flannels, black pumps, a silk shirt, a green laurel-wreath. Fair hair, and a golden battledore and shuttlecock. I am surprised that the audience did not throw things at me.

From *Early Stages*

The Insect Play, JG as Felix the poet butterfly, Regent Theatre, 1923

WENDY TOYE

I was twelve years old.

It was my first professional job, which meant that I was getting paid for it.

I was Moth in *A Midsummer Night's Dream* at the Old Vic, directed by Harcourt Williams.

The year was 1929.

In the cast were Margaret Webster, Donald Wolfit, Martita Hunt, Gyles Isham, Adele Dixon and John Gielgud as Oberon.

I had to say 'And I' and 'Hail'.

I had done that fairly satisfactorily and it came to the last scene. The Four Fairies had to collect their lanterns from the property room, then go to the stage management, who put a wad of cotton wool in the lanterns, which were on a little pole. The wads of cotton wool were then saturated with some very flammable liquid, lit with a match and we carried our lanterns with great care upstage, ready for our entrance.

On we came with our lanterns held high above our heads and we made a sort of arch for Oberon's entrance.

He entered looking magnificent and I can remember trembling with nerves. We all had to bow to him. I did this a little too energetically and my wad of cotton wool bounced out of my lantern on to Oberon's flowing cape, setting it, if not exactly alight, dangerously smouldering. He bravely travelled a couple of times round the stage but eventually decided to go off and be stamped out.

Now Sir John, very good-humouredly, denies all this when we meet:

'No no, my dear. You've imagined it all.'

But I hadn't, because after the play was over that night, I was summoned to Miss Lillian Baylis's office. She was very cross.

'Wendy,' she said, 'you must be punished.'

I thought that the Black Maria would be arriving at any moment to clap me into jail.

'You have been very careless and I must discipline you, dear. I will have to dock your salary.'

And she did. It was 3s 6d a performance.

I cannot fail to be constantly aware of my own narrow limitations. For me the theatre has always been an escape, a make-believe, full of colour and excitement, fun, emotion, poetry and movement, a world of striking characters and extraordinary personalities. I cannot bring myself to care for elaborate dialectic argument on the stage.

JOHN GIELGUD

Macbeth, Old Vic, 1930

Macbeth

JAMES AGATE

After being completely captivated by the first act of the play in 1930, James Agate went backstage during the interval to congratulate Gielgud:

'I only want to tell you that the murder scene was the best I have ever seen. I know you can't keep it up to the end of the play so I've come round now to tell you.'

But he was wrong, as he goes on to describe the rest of the evening in his review:

'Macbeth's next appearance is with Seyton, and whether the play is to stand or fall depends upon the power of the actor to suggest the ravages of mind, soul, and even body endured since we saw him last. Mr Gielgud did not begin again as so many Macbeths do, but came on the stage as though he had lived the interval . . . in the old phrase, the actor carried us away.'

From his review

EXQUISITE
GIELGUDRY

JAMES AGATE

Richard of Bordeaux, JG as Richard, New Theatre, 1933

Richard of Bordeaux

JOHN GIELGUD

The notices were enthusiastic the following morning, and I spent the day thanking people who telephoned me their congratulations. Several friends came round to my dressing-room after the second night, and there were compliments and a general feeling of optimism. The cheerful temperature in the room fell several degrees, however, when I opened the return for the performance and found that there had been only £77 in the house. Such modest takings did not indicate the great success which some people had so confidently predicted. The tide turned at the first matinée. Business had been quiet all the morning, and, at one o'clock, Mr Chatley, who is in charge of the box office at the New Theatre, told his assistant that he might go out to lunch. At ten minutes past one the telephone bell began to ring. Queues formed outside the theatre, and so great and unexpected was the rush that it was a quarter-past three before all the members of that afternoon's audience were in their seats.

From that moment *Richard of Bordeaux* became what the Americans call a 'smash hit'. I travelled down to Brighton for the day on the following Sunday, and although I was physically dog-tired, I felt so happy and exhilarated that I went for a long walk on the Downs in a heavy snowstorm.

From *Early Stages*

LAURENCE OLIVIER

In 1933, when he was acting in *Richard of Bordeaux*, Gielgud had some minor voice trouble and consulted Fogerty. She at once sat him down and told him to imagine that his head was a pot of marmalade that could communicate a kind of oozy relaxation to every muscle in his body. For reasons Gielgud never fathomed, the advice worked.

[Elsie Fogerty was one of the most celebrated voice teachers of her day.]

From *Laurence Olivier*

EMLYN WILLIAMS

Richard of Bordeaux being in its seventh month, its star was given two weeks' holiday, 'to make a break', took a suite in the Royal Crescent, Brighton, littered it with scripts, and asked me and Dick [Clowes] down for a couple of days.

He went for walks between us along the front, the ozone fertilizing his mind with ideas while his eyes spotted theatre faces with the excitement of a Gallery First-Nighter. 'I've got rather a good idea for *A Midsummer Night's Dream* – to do it nude, or as near as one could go – wouldn't it be superb?'

He made it sound just that, till he added, 'With everybody starkers we could just call it "Bottom",' and shrieked with nursery laughter . . .

One rainy afternoon he decided on a night out in London. By now I knew him well enough to guess that he would take us to a theatre, but not well enough to know which one.

After a fine early dinner at the Café Royal, Dick and I found ourselves sitting in the front of a stage box, with the holiday-maker lurking in the shadows. We were at the New Theatre, watching *Richard of Bordeaux*, 'I'm curious to see it from the front.'

As the theatre darkened Dick whispered to me, 'Would you call this "making a break"?'

Glen Byam Shaw was playing Richard as a rehearsal for his tour in the part, and playing well. At the end of one emotional scene between the king and his wife, I stole a look behind me: John G was not just moved, he was weeping. I was in the company of a child playing with double mirrors.

When at the end we hurried through the pass-door, the stage-hands stacking scenery looked through the visitor without recognizing him. They had plainly never seen him in a suit.

Glen was staggered – 'Thank God I didn't know' – and delighted by praise generous and sincere. Then John took Dick and me out to supper as if after a first night he had enjoyed.

Dick said, 'John dear, I know the play moved you, but I did once see you lean forward and count the house through your tears.'

'Dickie Clowes, that's a wicked thing to say. Actually it wasn't at all bad, I was surprised . . .'

From *Emlyn*

WILLIAM FOX

During the run of *Richard of Bordeaux* at the New Theatre (as it then was) the Motleys (sets and costumes) gave a big party for Johnny G at their workshop home, off St Martin's Lane behind the Garrick Club. All the stars of the West End were there.

Some time after midnight, Edith Evans, Sybil Thorndike and Ellis Jefferies got up to go home. They approached John to say goodnight. He was playing the piano. He didn't stop playing, he didn't get up, merely lifted one limp hand from the keyboard and extended it to be kissed by each actress in turn – a right royal gesture!

JACK HAWKINS

Throughout those last few years before the war I always seemed to gravitate back to John Gielgud. I first worked with him in his production of *Richard of Bordeaux*, when I took over the part of the Earl of Oxford from Francis Lister. A few months after I joined, the production celebrated its first anniversary, and of course there were a large number of *aficionados* at the front of the house.

At the end of the performance there were cries of 'Speech, speech!' and Johnny stepped forward. He thanked the audience for its support, and said: 'I know that many of you have been to see us thirty or forty times.' He paused, and looked along the line of the cast, searching for words. His eyes lighted on me, and he added: 'In spite of the changes in the cast.'

From *Anything For a Quiet Life*

ANTHONY QUAYLE

Of the *Richard* rehearsals I remember how struck I was by John's elegant clothes – his suede shoes, his beautifully cut suits, his immaculate shirts, the long gold key chain that went around his waist before diving into a trouser pocket; I had never seen the like. I remember how courteous he was to the older and very distinguished members of his cast – and well he may have been: though God-like to me in his eminence, he was only twenty-eight.

From *A Time to Speak*

If you shut down all the power stations in Britain, you could hardly lose more electricity than went out when he stopped playing in Gordon Daviot's *Richard of Bordeaux* in 1934.

HAROLD HOBSON

I wonder whether John is a *great* actor. His grace and poise are remarkable, and his voice would melt the entire Inland Revenue.

JAMES AGATE

Noah, New Theatre, 1935

JOHN GIELGUD ON CRITICISM

It's – wonderful – when –
it – isn't – you.

Romeo and Juliet

Romeo and Juliet, JG as Mercutio, New Theatre, 1935

Laurence Olivier as Romeo and Peggy Ashcroft as Juliet

GEOFFREY TOONE

Picture the ballroom scene in *Romeo and Juliet* (cast included Olivier, Peggy Ashcroft, Edith Evans, Alec Guinness, George Devine and me as Tybalt. Programme (*3d*) which I still have – riveting advertisements – Tweed Coat and Skirt from Marshall & Snelgrove £3 10*s*). The final dress rehearsal in progress. Capulet welcomes the guests in jovial manner, ending, 'Give room and foot it girls' (music plays and they dance) which indeed they did beautifully choreographed by Chattie Saloman, Merula Guinness's sister. Capulet chunters merrily on, Romeo sees Juliet – *coup de foudre* – 'Oh she doth Teach the torches to burn bright' etc. Tybalt is tucked in a corner down stage right, glowering morosely. He sees Romeo and is considerably displeased: 'This by his voice Should be a Montague,' he cries, 'Fetch me my rapier, boy,' and more in the same vein.

There was nothing in those days to stop rehearsals going on far into the night and this one did. Tybalt's cue was his seeing and hearing Romeo, so what with mistakes in the dancing or the music or the dialogue his cue never occurred on time and he could scarcely cry 'This by his voice Should be a Montague' if Romeo was miles away out of his sight or hearing, not having been able to arrive at his appointed place. After several unsuccessful dry runs, John's voice rang out from the auditorium 'I'm sorry, everyone – I know it's late and you're all tired but Geoffrey has got it wrong *again* and we'll have to go back to the beginning of the dance once *more.*'

Next day, more in sorrow than in anger I said to John, 'You know it wasn't my fault that we had to keep going back.' 'Yes I know, dear,' he replied, 'but we're such old friends, so I knew you wouldn't mind.' Which I expect I didn't.

JG ON OLIVIER

The only trouble came in our scenes together, when we kept on trying to speak on each other's cues.

Gwen Ffrangcon-Davies recalled how unhappy both Olivier and I were in tights. Olivier because his legs were so thin and me because I was so knock-kneed.

JOHN GIELGUD

When I first worked with Laurence Olivier in *Romeo and Juliet* [in 1935], we alternated the parts of Mercutio and Romeo. I was directing and I bullied him a great deal about his verse-speaking, which, he admitted himself, he wasn't happy about. I was rather showy about mine, and fancied myself very much a verse-speaker, and I became very mannered in consequence. But I was so jealous, because not only did he play Romeo with tremendous energy but he knew just how to cope with it and select. I remember Ralph Richardson saying to me, 'But you see, when Larry leans against the balcony and looks up, then you have the whole scene, immediately.' Because he has this wonderful plastique, which is absolutely unselfconscious, like a lithe panther or something. I had been draping myself around the stage for weeks, thinking myself very romantic as Romeo, and I was rather baffled and dismayed that I couldn't achieve the same effect at all.

ALAN DENT

Mr Gielgud was his own Mercutio and produced him at least as well as anybody or anything else. The part was spoken with rare virtuosity. Pater has said that the greatest art tends to escape into the condition of music. It was so last night. With this actor's delivery of the Queen Mab lines they become a scherzo, the words fluttering from Mercutio's brain as lightly as the elfin vision that they drew.

From *Preludes and Studies*

IVOR BROWN

Mr Gielgud has the most meaningless legs imaginable.

The Secret Agent

JOHN GIELGUD

In *Secret Agent* I lay for several days under iron girders and rubbish in a scene of a train wreck. Another day I sat for hours before a blank screen, while a short length of Lake Como was unrolled behind me in 'back-projection', a device which enables studio scenes to be played before backgrounds of places hundreds of miles away. A very wonderful process, but utterly boring for the actors to endure, as the photographed background sticks and goes wrong, and has to be rewound twenty times before it runs so as to last exactly the requisite amount of time.

From *Early Stages*

Peter Lorre was very naughty on *Secret Agent*. He was rather a fascinating little man, also a morphine maniac. He used to go up and hide in the roof of the studio and have a fix.

He was a great scene stealer. I didn't know you could steal scenes on the screen but he was very good at it. He'd put in one extra line at the end of a scene which hadn't been rehearsed, or suddenly take a step up or down stage so that the camera would stay with him rather than me.

The Secret Agent, JG as Ashenden,
Peter Lorre as The Mexican, 1936

Richard II, Queen's Theatre, 1937

Richard II

HAROLD HOBSON

The royalty of speech, the tension of nerves, the overriding of all rational emotion by the torrential or elegiac beauty of words and images which are more evident in Richard than in any other of Shakespeare's characters, was exactly suited to Gielgud's temperament. It was with a terrible majesty, charged with an anger controlled only by a superhuman effort, that Gielgud spoke Richard's rebuke of outraged majesty when Northumberland did not kneel to him.

From *Theatre in Britain: A Personal View*

Tall willowy figure in black velvet, surmounted by a fair head, the pale agonized face set beneath a glittering crown.

HARCOURT WILLIAMS

Gielgud gave the best light comic performance I've ever seen.

LAURENCE OLIVIER

The School for Scandal, Alec Guinness as Snake

The School for Scandal

JG as Joseph Surface, Queen's Theatre, 1937

RALPH MICHAEL

Sir John has been my major theatrical hero since his performance of Hamlet in 1930 at the Old Vic. I saw him do it three times. Not in 1928, but as he grew stronger in the character, and illuminated certain passages with dazzling wit, humour, and perception; making ice-clear the meaning, to people like myself, whom he mesmerized in Shakespeare's name.

Sir John produced *The Heiress*, and when I took over the part of Morris Townsend from James Donald at the Theatre Royal, Haymarket, with Peggy Ashcroft and Ralph Richardson, he rehearsed me conscientiously and thoroughly. While we were waiting for Charles Peace, the stage manager, to return from lunch, Gielgud was pacing the stage down by the floats while I talked to Gillian Lind in the darkened area up stage. I hoped John could hear my chatter, so told Gillian I had done 'years of Shakespeare', but lacked the musical tones to do it well, and 'my feet were too big'. 'Of course,' I said; 'I could have them cut off, and walk on the ends of my legs.' A thin but tolerant smile curled Gielgud's lip as he murmured without stopping his walk: 'Why don't you? It's perfectly possible.'

My next encounter with him was at the Globe Theatre in *Medea*, with Eileen Herlie. As Jason, her husband, I was clad in an heroic golden cuirass shaped to fit my body, but bigger. This made my arms seem shorter, and Gielgud complained at the dress rehearsal; 'Rayf, dear boy, if you can't do gestures, keep your arms by your sides, or you look like a signal box.' Whatever his opinion of the play, in which he had played Jason in New York, he was loyal to us, his team of actors, in London. About once a week Gielgud walked elegantly into my dressing-room at the Globe, and announced to whatever friends I had in the room: 'Rayf is wonderful as Jason. I played it myself in New York, and know how difficult it is. He brings something to it that I could never do.'

My first wife, Fay Compton, played Gertrude to John's Hamlet during the Second World War, and toured England when the land was blacked out. During a Sunday train journey in a compartment reserved for the company, Gielgud quietly made up words to fit *The Times* crossword puzzle, and the rest of them argued about Turkey coming into the war, and if so, on whose side. The debate reached an impasse. 'What do you think, John?' they asked him. 'About what?' said John. 'Should Turkey come into the war?' Gielgud moved his newspaper aside: 'Are they keen?' he enquired.

Hamlet

JOHN GIELGUD

When we took *Hamlet* to Elsinore I had a very tiresome fan who followed me there. She and a friend used to move their seats during the course of the play so that they could sit opposite me. So one night I changed all my moves to evade them, much to the frustration and bewilderment of my fellow players.

The next day one of them came up to our table, where we were having dinner, and said, 'I've translated all the notices for you – I thought you would like to see them in English.' She then handed me a large sheet of paper which, like a fool, I started to read out loud.

Suddenly I heard myself, with all the company sitting around, saying, 'Miss Compton has neither the looks or the youth of Ophelia, but obviously comes from good theatrical stock.'

Fay was wonderful. She roared with laughter and took it straight on the chin. But it taught me never to read *anything* out loud without having read it first.

FABIA DRAKE

I asked him at his party afterwards what had guided the arrow at this unique performance right into the heart of Hamlet?

'I went out alone this afternoon,' he said, 'to Richmond Park.'

And that was all he said.

From *Blind Fortune*

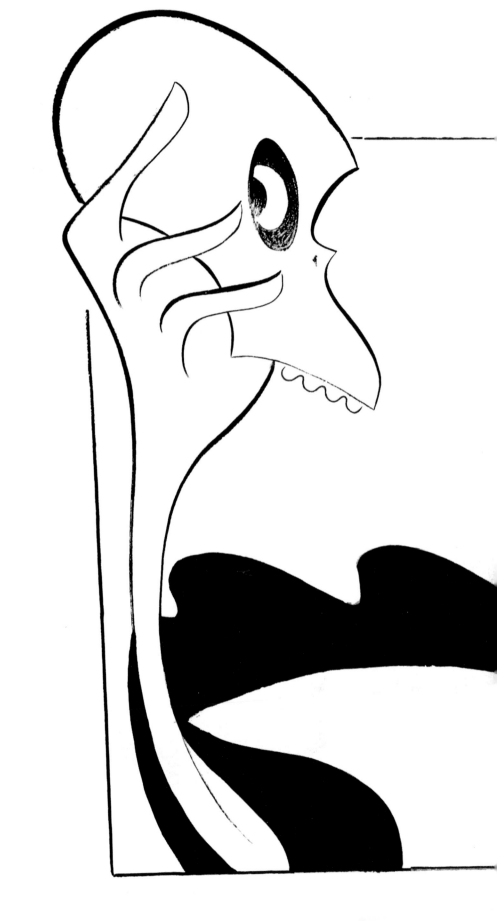

JG as Hamlet, New Theatre 1934; Elsinore 1939; Theatre Royal, Haymarket, 1944

ALEC GUINNESS

It was after a week of rehearsing *Hamlet* that he spoke 'spontaneously' to me, with shattering effect. 'What's happened to you?' he cried. 'I thought you were rather good. You're terrible. Oh, go away! I don't want to see you again!'

I hung around at rehearsals until the end of the day and then approached him cautiously. 'Excuse me, Mr Gielgud, but am I fired?'

'No! Yes! No, of course not. But go away. Come back in a week. Get someone to teach you how to act. Try Martita Hunt.'

From *Blessings in Disguise*

BERNARD LEVIN

After seeing John Gielgud's last Hamlet at the Haymarket Theatre in 1944, I walked all the way home, a distance of some four miles, without being in any way conscious of my surroundings until I found myself, to my extreme astonishment, putting my key in the door.

SIR CEDRIC HARDWICKE

Sir Cedric Hardwicke recalled in his entertaining memoirs that he had the most intense conversations about the theatre with New York cabbies. One time, he asked what one of them thought of John Gielgud's Hamlet which was then the talk of the town.

'I don't care for the name,' said the cabbie.

'You mean Gielgud?' asked Hardwicke.

'No, Hamlet.'

From *Broadway Anecdotes*

John Gielgud went backstage after the opening night of Olivier's *Hamlet*. 'Larry, it's one of the finest performances I have ever seen, but it's still my part.'

CLAIRE BLOOM

I'll never forget seeing him in *Hamlet* in 1946 – the picture of him, sitting in his chair: he had a white square collar insert and the black tunic and this long, long neck, and wonderful elevated head and piercing blue eyes – eyes piercing with intelligence. Then there was his voice, the most lyrical voice that's ever been heard on the English stage. Lyrical, yet guided always by intelligence. Then there's that tremendous nervous tension you feel with him all the time. And so delicate: subtle, sensitive, and open to everything around him. And, of course, tasteful to a degree. I think he's the greatest Hamlet we'll ever see, I should think the greatest Hamlet that's ever been.

From *Limelight and After*

The Importance of
Being Earnest

The Importance of Being Earnest, JG as John Worthing, Globe, 1939

JOHN GIELGUD

When I first thought of asking Edith [Evans] to do *The Importance of Being Earnest*, she came down to the cottage I had in Essex in those days. We took the play out of the bookcase and read the handbag scene together. At the end we all laughed and thought it was so marvellous and she shut the book and said, 'I know that kind of woman. She rings the bell and asks you to put another lump of coal on.'

King Lear
ANDREW CRUICKSHANK

I remember once during the rehearsal of the last scene with Gloucester, Gielgud, standing not far from me in the stalls with his minute copy of the play, squinnying at something he'd written then shouting out, 'Barker told me that I should play this scene as though there was a pain shooting through my head!' Later, when the play had been running some time, Peggy Ashcroft and I were standing in the wings watching this scene. Then at the words 'This a good block', John slowly dipped his head against the head of the blind Gloucester, for all the world as I used to press my head against the cold glass of the window if I had a headache. We both shivered for a moment. The theatre is wonderful when it reveals its depths spontaneously.

From *Andrew Cruickshank: An Autobiography*

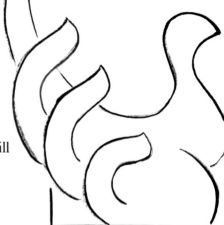

HARLEY GRANVILLE-BARKER

Lear is an oak. You are an ash. We must see how this will serve you.

King Lear, Old Vic, 1940

Macbeth
CONSTANCE CUMMINGS

He was a wonderful Macbeth. This play is something of an enigma and a hurdle for actors. (Perhaps this is the explanation for the tradition in the theatre that it is an 'unlucky' play.) William Macready, a famous tragedian and a very successful Macbeth, recorded in his diary one night, 'A good performance this evening, after forty years of playing this part, I think I now know how to approach it.'

I remember, years ago, when Laurence Olivier heard that Michael Redgrave was going into rehearsal with Macbeth, he smiled sympathetically and said, 'Well, there's another young, aspiring actor who is going to find that part is unplayable.'

John transcended whatever difficulties have plagued other actors in this part. He played it at a tempo which swept the tragedy along irresistibly, from the moment in Act I, scene 5 when he swept onto the stage and embraced his wife and they had the short exchange which revealed that both knew what great things the future could hold for them.

His Macbeth was primarily a man of action and the occasional misgivings of the character were not allowed to turn him from his purpose. This gave the play an underlying tension of which he was always in command.

I think John and Shakespeare have much in common. The few descriptions we have of Shakespeare's character from his contemporaries assure us that he was a man of wit . . . of a sweet disposition . . . always a pleasant, courteous companion . . . he was highly esteemed by his contemporaries in and out of the theatre . . . all this is said of John.

As author and as actor they share the mysterious gift of using words to take us into realms of awareness and understanding where paraphrase is dumb.

Macbeth, Piccadilly Theatre, 1942

Love for Love
ROBERT FLEMING

Being the all-round man of the theatre that he is, Sir John is not only a great actor, but also a most distinguished director. He has directed a great many successful productions, including many, but by no means all, of the plays in which he himself was appearing.

In the pursuit of perfection, however, he is famous among the older members of our profession for his propensity constantly to change moves right up to the final dress rehearsal – and sometimes beyond.

On one occasion we were playing a week in Washington with Congreve's *Love for Love* prior to opening in New York the following week. In those days, plays of this period were apt to finish with the entire cast mincing around in circles waving lace handkerchiefs in each other's faces in a sort of gavotte, and we were about to come to the end of the Wednesday matinée. I found myself placed in one of the circles up stage left as was Sir John. As I was about to pass him – frantically waving my handkerchief in order to impress – he said in a whisper of that famous voice that could have been heard in Baltimore, 'Get down stage *right*.' After a moment's hesitation I dutifully pushed my way through the somewhat startled cast to down stage right and I started to wave my handkerchief in the face of the nearest astonished actor.

The curtain came down and after the calls, Sir John, without a word, proceeded to hurry towards his dressing-room at considerable speed. However, I managed to catch up with him and said, 'Surely, John, I was not in the wrong place, was I?'

To which Sir John – without pausing in his stride for one second and all in one breath – said, 'I thought it might be better there – it isn't.'

Gielgud as Valentine postured
beautifully. Tongue-in-cheek and
hand-on-heart,
he played the mock-madness
scenes as a sort of burlesque
of his own Hamlet.
Gielgud is an actor who refuses
to compromise with his
audience: he does not offer a
welcoming hand, but
binds a spell instead.

KENNETH TYNAN
From his review

Love for Love, JG as Valentine,
Theatre Royal Haymarket, 1944

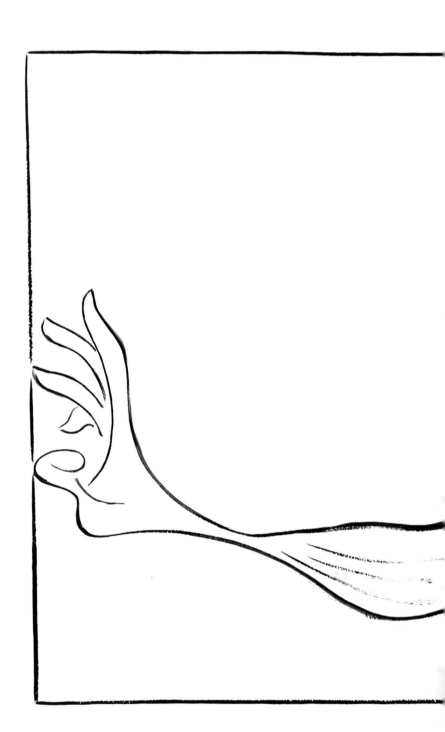

The Lady's Not for Burning

The Lady's Not for Burning, Pamela Brown as Jennet Jourdemayne

CHRISTOPHER FRY

At a performance of *The Lady's Not for Burning*, John made a spoonerism in the line:
'Ask that neighing horsebox-kicker there, your matchless brother!' which became:
'Ask that neighing matchbox-kicker there, your horseless brother!'
I re-titled the play to myself as *The Neighing Matchbox*.

Richard Burton as Richard, JG as Thomas Mendip, Globe Theatre, 1949

ROBERT HARDY

Stratford 1949: sitting by the half-open door in one of the old dressing-rooms on the second floor; a new recruit, studying the art of make-up, all by myself; a door opened upstairs, the theatre manager's door; two voices, one was Gielgud's; the hair prickled on the back of my neck: 'Straight down three flights, along the corridor to the stage door . . . goodbye.' The door closed; footsteps. Then: 'Down, down I come like glist'ring Phaethon, wanting the manage of unruly jades.' The minor cadences, the cello cry from the highest notes flighting down to lowest vibrations powerfully bowed, in the empty corridors, and I had the luck to be there. Gielgud was playing *The Lady's Not For Burning* in London, in the mornings directing *Much Ado About Nothing* at Stratford. I had not yet met him, the greatest actor in England, and therefore in the world!

London 1952: 'Why don't you come and play Claudio for me?' I joined his company for the record-breaking run of *Much Ado* at the Phoenix. Gielgud's Benedick, Wynyard's Beatrice, Scofield's Don Pedro, Tutin's Hero, Lewis Casson, George Rose, Brewster Mason. . . . After a night out, I overslept, and woke thirty-five minutes before a matinée two miles away; got a taxi, arrived at the Phoenix ten minutes before curtain up, sweating, quaking, dry-mouthed. Gielgud said, almost with a grin, 'There you are . . . rather naughty . . . take your time.' They held the curtain. Half ready in the wings, like a walking corpse, I heard his voice behind me: 'Try not to worry . . . do relax . . . and remember to think of me as Benedick, not John Gielgud . . . it will never do you know if you are all tense and hunched . . . just think of yourself as a Renaissance princeling . . . take a leaf out of my book.'

That evening, before the last entrance, he said: 'Come and have some gin . . . not too much . . . mustn't be pissy-assed for the dance . . . there . . . what a horrid day for you . . . I think, you know, in the church scene you should try. . . .' On another occasion during the run; in the masked ball, Don John pretends to mistake Claudio for Benedick. In my reply, 'You know me well, I am he', I used to imitate Gielgud, which I've always been able to do pretty well. On a good night, with Gielgud fans abounding, I would get a laugh. This night I had a huge one. Next entrance made for a small crowd of us under the stage. As I arrived to take my place, I heard Gielgud in conversation with the group: '. . . good mimics are very seldom good actors.' I was properly crestfallen.

Oxford 1992: after a long and tough day, plagued by bad weather and bad light, filming the last *Inspector Morse*, Gielgud playing the chancellor of the university: ten of us sitting, waiting, at seven in the evening in a don's room in Trinity, Gielgud looking tired. The first assistant came in: 'Sir John we're up against it; would you mind if we went on till nine?' Gielgud said, 'Yes, but please not beyond ten, or I shall never appear in the morning,' and leant back on the sofa with his eyes closed. A conversation started up, and I put a finger to my lips to quieten it. Silence. Gielgud, suddenly awake and vivid, and referring to the snatch of conversation: 'How odd that you should say that; Larry, you know, absolutely refused once . . .' and with perfect recall there followed a brilliant cascade of stories, some more than risqué, jewels of wit and judgement gleaming among them.

That total recall, that mercurial and incisive mind, that speed of thought; the kindness and generosity; the clear judgement. The poise; sometimes the impatience – 'Oh, do try to be funny, George!'; the passion: I sat in the Stratford stalls the day he first allowed himself full rein in rehearsal as Cassius, and was afraid at the vehemence. The most genuine and beguiling humility, hand in hand with a marvellous arrogance, a sort of royalty. May the king live for ever.

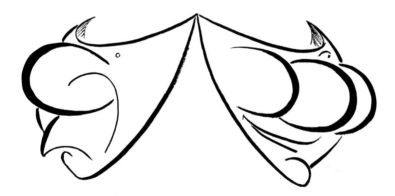

Much Ado About Nothing

JOHN MOFFATT

JG's production of *Much Ado* had had an immensely successful run at Stratford and in 1952 H M Tennent's brought the production to the Phoenix Theatre with a largely new cast but with JG playing Benedick of course and with George Rose repeating his celebrated Dogberry. I (although very young at the time) was playing Verges. One night, after we had given about a hundred performances, Mr Gielgud (as he then was) said, 'These Watch scenes are getting dreadfully common. Send all the costumes to the cleaners and George . . . take that terrible nose off and wear a ring!'

The next day the costumes, which had previously been very carefully 'broken down', came back from the cleaners in sparkling colours, George put on a juvenile make-up in place of the splendidly grotesque one he had worn so far, the members of the Watch looked like chorus boys . . . all eyes and teeth . . . and Verges had shed about fifty years. George also sported an immense ruby ring. Naturally the character voices had to go and we all played the scene in the accents of a genteel vicarage tea party. Gielgud stood in the wings watching with tears of laughter running down his cheeks and, after the curtain call, he turned to us and said, 'It doesn't really work, does it? I think we'll go back to what we did yesterday.' I've often wondered what the audience on that particular occasion made of it.

PEGGY ASHCROFT

Describing their partnership in Much Ado About Nothing: 'It was like following your partner so that you never quite knew which steps you were going to take but you could always respond since you were so in tune.'

CONSTANCE CUMMINGS

'. . . one man in his time plays many parts . . .' and how fortunate are those who have been able to watch John Gielgud do just that. What marvellous memories of these authors – Shakespeare, Sheridan, Ibsen, Chekhov, Barrie, Shaw, Maugham, Coward, Christopher Fry, Edward Albee, Harold Pinter, David Storey – because John has played them.

Who could forget the moment in *Much Ado About Nothing* when Benedick has been tricked into overhearing a planned conversation which convinces him that Beatrice is only pretending disdain and she is really in love with him.

The conspirators leave and Benedick comes from behind the hedge that has concealed him and goes into a soliloquy in which he finds for himself one reason after another why he should reform his opinion of Beatrice. He blames himself for being churlish, he finds a series of things to be said in her favour, he admits to himself that he has a few bad points, he knows he is proud . . . well, he can mend his character etc, etc, until he ends with a marvellous combination of chagrin, awareness that he has not made a watertight case for his character, a tinge of amusement that he finds himself in a position that is less than flattering, and finally ends with an attempt at defiance by saying, 'When I said I would die a bachelor I did not think that I should live till I were married.'

Much Ado About Nothing, JG as Benedick

Peggy Ashcroft as Beatrice, Stratford, 1950

DOROTHY TUTIN

I was thrilled to be offered Hero when John's famous production of *Much Ado About Nothing* came from Stratford to London. I had been told he always had many ideas so it was best to be 'open' to anything. He was quite brilliant as Benedick, the wittiest I have ever seen but the Hero scene tricking Beatrice that Benedick was in love with her obviously bored him as much as it terrified me. Finally, he exploded in exasperation and said, 'Oh dear, this is all dreadfully *dull* – give the poor girl a fan – or something.' I was presented with a period thing and waved it about and he said, 'Oh good. That's *much better*' and never another note I had.

CURT DEHN

John Gielgud, it's a rum sort of head. The profile's Roman Emperor, but the rest is still at Eton.

James Agate's lawyer

What a possession
for any theatre!
It is irrelevant to say
that he was fair in this
part, good in that, brilliant
in that; Gielgud is more
important than the
sum of his parts.

KENNETH TYNAN
From his review

The Way of the World

NOËL COWARD

Saturday 4 April 1953
The Way of the World – brilliantly directed by
John Gielgud and, although to me largely in-
comprehensible, the play was so well done that
after the first act I enjoyed it.

From *The Noël Coward Diaries*

The Way of the World, JG as Mirabel, Lyric Theatre, Hammersmith, 1953

Venice Preserv'd

PAUL SCOFIELD

In 1952 I was taking part in the John Gielgud season at the Lyric Theatre, Hammersmith. The last of the three plays presented was *Venice Preserv'd* by Thomas Otway, directed by Peter Brook and designed by Leslie Hurry. John's first appearance came early in the play, when he spoke a long soliloquy. At the end of the speech I was to make my first entrance.

On one particular evening John appeared and began to speak. He was immediately engulfed in the most startling and tumultuous ovation that I have ever heard. From my vantage point in the wings it seemed to me that the whole audience was on its feet. I could see John facing them, his stance typical, head thrown up; and from the waist up, his body leaning slightly backward, feet placed perfectly, like a dancer.

He couldn't speak because they wouldn't let him and he also couldn't speak because the tears were coursing down his face. After what seemed an interminable length of time the house gradually quietened and John, still choked with emotion, delivered his speech with more than his usual poignancy. I, as Pierre, intruded into this extraordinary scene and the play continued as usual.

It was, needless to say, the day on which John became Sir John, and the tribute paid to him by the audience on that night is engraved in my memory.

Venice Preserv'd, JG as Jaffeir, Lyric Theatre, Hammersmith, 1953

DULCIE GRAY

John's contribution to the theatre of the last sixty years has been unique. Besides being a very great Shakespearean actor with a voice of incomparable music, and a dazzling gift for illuminating the parts he plays, he has given his great contemporaries crucial opportunities to fulfil their potential. Laurence Olivier, Peggy Ashcroft, Edith Evans, Alec Guinness, Michael Redgrave and Paul Scofield all owed him a great debt.

The theatre I came into over fifty years ago was very largely light-weight. John, with Binkie Beaumont's help, spurred it into something much more cerebral.

I first met him in 1943 when he directed me in a play called *Landslide* and like all of us without exception I became devoted. Not the least of his lovable traits is humility. Rather breathtaking in view of his Olympian achievements.

Two short stories: Michael [Denison] – then under contract to Associated British Films – told his boss Robert Clark that *The Importance of Being Earnest* would shortly be out of copyright. Robert bought it at the first opportunity and asked Michael and me to take John out to dinner to try to persuade him to direct it as a film. We took him to the Ivy and very nervously put the question to him.

He replied gently, 'Oh no. I don't think so. I seem to have been doing the play for years and years. I don't think it would make a film, do you?' A pause – then, 'Of course it might be rather fun to do it Chinese.'

A suggestion which did not commend itself to the film company!

When he was directing *The Trojans* at Covent Garden, he kindly invited me to sit in at a rehearsal. It was the first time that the Trojan horse itself (a huge wooden structure) was to be tried out. John attempted to whip up the Chorus to feelings of violent passion, curiosity, fear and horror. After a short talk on the subject he asked for the music to be played for the arrival of the horse. The great machine made a majestic arrival, but to John's dismay, the chorus showed little emotion of any kind. After a second or two of complete amazement, John leapt down the aisle of the auditorium towards the stage. 'No! No! No!' he shouted in exasperation. 'That won't do! That won't do at all! You look as if you are seeing not very good friends off from Waterloo!'

JOYCE GRENFELL

February 2nd, 1941
Lying in the bath on Friday night with the radio on to a programme called *The Curtain Goes Up*, about theatre questions, I heard John Gielgud being interviewed and asked if he thought theatre was make-believe or reality (or should be either of these things) and he said it was half and half to most actors 'but to brilliant people like Ruth Draper and Joyce Grenfell it was make-believe'. (We 'people' the stage, it seems!) I nearly fell down the drain in my pleasure at such a tribute from such a person.

From *Joyce Grenfell: Darling Ma*

EMLYN WILLIAMS

Regarding Emlyn Williams's ill-fated Spring 1600, *which John Gielgud directed in 1934 at the Shaftesbury Theatre:* Gielgud directed the production with a sensitiveness that brought to life a long-lost spring of centuries ago. 'I'm happy to have done it whatever happens,' said Gielgud. 'You've been so patient, it's a lovely play.' On the first night Emlyn skulked nervously high up in the flies amid ropes and pulleys. From the distant stage below he heard the swirl of the curtain, the faint snatches of music, the murmur of voices speaking lines he knew by heart. A sudden desperate need overcame him and he relieved it in a dusty old wash-basin. 'You must,' said Gielgud later when he told him, 'be the first playwright who's peed over his own play.'

From *Emlyn Williams: A Life*

I suppose it is natural as I grow older for me to find it difficult to repress a certain amount of nostalgia for the theatre of my youth . . . but I have learned, and have, I hope, much more to learn, from the younger generation of playwrights, directors, and especially the actors with whom I now come in contact for the first time.

JOHN GIELGUD

LAURENCE OLIVIER

[A few days after Olivier's first performance of *Richard III* at the Old Vic in 1944] . . . a long, slender package was delivered, addressed to Olivier from John Gielgud. Beneath a dozen roses was history's most famous theatrical memento: the sword worn by Edmund Kean as Richard in 1814, which had passed down through two generations of actors to Henry Irving in 1877. Irving had bequeathed it to William Terriss (a member of his company), who was murdered in 1897. His daughter (the actress Ellaline Terriss) later passed it on to her husband, the actor-manager Seymour Hicks, and eventually it reached the Terry family. On its blade that September evening was a new inscription: 'This sword given him by his mother Kate Terry Gielgud, 1938, is given to Laurence Olivier by his friend John Gielgud in appreciation of his performance of *Richard III* at the New Theatre, 1944.' When asked in 1979 to whom he would bequeath it, Olivier replied, 'No one. It's mine.' And so it remained. He made no provision in his will for disposition of the sword.

From *Laurence Olivier*

JOHN JUSTIN

'I was very shy. The trouble was that John Gielgud was as shy as me, and we used to pace up and down behind the set waiting for our entrance. He never said a word and I never dared speak to him. One evening, after we'd been running for about three months, he tried to say something which came out as if he was clearing his throat, "errr . . . errr . . . uhmmmm . . . mm . . . erhhhaaahhh . . ." I tried to say something back but I couldn't get it out. However, it did break the ice. A week later he managed to say "Good evening" and so did I. A month later this progressed to "Good evening, how are you?" nearly a whole sentence, and by the end of the run we were almost carrying on a conversation. After a year we became rather friendly and later we did become very close.'

From *Binkie Beaumont*

Julius Caesar

MARLON BRANDO

[Joseph] Mankiewicz's appreciation of fine acting led him to cast John Gielgud as Cassius, the chief conspirator in Caesar's assassination. One of the noblest of Britain's titled actors, Gielgud is especially revered for the bravura precision of his vocal technique. Cadaverously thin, with the sharp, deceptively benign features of a hooded falcon, he was the ideal 'lean and hungry' Cassius, and the role had brought him enormous acclaim on the British stage.

Hollywood society preened itself for Gielgud's visit [in 1955], the social occasion of the season; in anticipation, the Beverly Hills hostesses decanted the sherry, dressed up the poolside buffets with the best silver and damask, and dusted off the butler from central casting. Brando was as excited as everyone else, but he didn't attend any of the galas; he wasn't interested in chatting with Gielgud, he wanted to watch him act.

As soon as rehearsals began, Marlon haunted the set, surreptitiously appearing whenever Gielgud was scheduled to read a scene. Once he asked the Englishman to record two of Antony's speeches on his tape recorder. Gielgud accepted, and was astonished to find Brando's dressing room a littered library of tapes and recordings of Laurence Olivier, John Barrymore, Maurice Evans, and Ralph Richardson. Marlon explained that he was studying these records to improve his diction.

'Brando's very deferential to me,' Gielgud wrote to a friend. 'He's a funny, intense, egocentric boy. . . . He's very nervous and mutters his lines and rehearses by himself all day long. . . . I think his sincerity may bring him to an interesting performance. His English is not at all bad . . . but I think he has very little sense of humour.'

Later Marlon asked Gielgud to advise him on the interpretation of a speech. Gielgud was reluctant to poach on what was clearly the director's terrain, but when Mankiewicz approved the tutelage, he readily coached Brando.

'Marlon's difficulty was that he didn't really know the whole play,' Gielgud said. 'But he was very quick . . . I talked to him for a couple of hours, and the next morning he came down to work, and he'd put in everything I'd suggested, and executed it most skilfully. I wasn't in any other scenes with him and the director never asked me to interfere again, and Marlon didn't ask me, so I didn't like to press it. I don't know whether I could have helped him.'

One day, Gielgud asked Brando, 'Why don't you play Hamlet?' Coming from one of the great Hamlets of the twentieth century, the question itself was a compliment.

From *Marlon Brando: The Only Contender*

HARRY ANDREWS

Some years before he went to Hollywood to make *Julius Caesar*, John performed the play at Stratford on Avon, I played Brutus, and in the conspiracy scene where Brutus plans to murder Caesar he says, 'Let us kill him boldly but not wrathfully, let us carve him as a dish fit for the Gods.' (Act 2, scene 1) but one night I got it wrong and said, 'Let us carve him as a fish dish for the Gods.' Fortunately it passed unnoticed by the audience but it nearly demolished the actors on stage!

John, not realising James's [Mason] problems with the giggles, recounted this story to him just before they were to film the scene together, and James corpsed every time – in the end they had to abandon shooting for the rest of the day. Now half a day's shooting represents an awful lot of money, and this must surely have been one of the most expensive giggles in the history of the cinema.

From Diana de Rosso,
James Mason: A Personal Biography

JAMES MASON

At one time, either during the shooting of the film or later, Gielgud said that he thought it might be fun sometime for the two of us to do the play again but with him playing Brutus and me playing Cassius. Indeed I would like to do that, though I cannot see Gielgud ever being able to justify Caesar's line, 'Let me have men about me that are fat.'
From *Before I Forget*

Julius Caesar, James Mason as Brutus

Marlon Brando as Mark Antony, 1953

King Lear, Stratford, 1955

GIELGUD ON CRYING

Edith Evans once said to me, very politely, that if I cried a little less the audience would cry a little more. Which was quite true. I used to flatter myself that my real tears were of such value.

But all the Terrys had them. My mother said she couldn't think why she cried so much at plays and the doctor said, 'Oh, just weak lachrymal glands, my dear.'

I once made a very unfortunate remark to a newspaper reporter when I said, 'Yes, I always burst into tears if I see a regiment marching or a queen passing.' Which wasn't quite the thing to say.

JOHN MILLS

In the late autumn Binkie Beaumont asked me to play a part I had first played in London in 1930 – the Aunt in *Charley's Aunt*. It was to be a prestigious production – no expense spared – with costumes by Cecil Beaton and Sir John Gielgud as director. I knew but had never worked with Johnny G, as he is affectionately called, and I looked forward enormously to the experience. I can't remember a dull moment. He has a wonderful sense of humour, and is famous for dropping the most marvellous clangers. My favourite moment was during the dress rehearsal at the Haymarket Theatre. Some plays are absolutely hellish to rehearse. *Charley's Aunt* is one of them: without an audience it seems to be just about the un-funniest piece ever written. I finished the first act pouring with sweat after tearing round the stage in the heavy black frock, wig and bonnet. Johnny G was out front in the stalls. There was dead silence. I walked to the footlights and, shading my eyes from the glare, peered out into the auditorium. 'Johnny,' I said, 'are you there?'

'Yes, I am.'

'Well . . . what did you think of it?'

'Interminable, my dear fellow, absolutely interminable.'

From *Up in the Clouds, Gentlemen Please*

Richard III JG as Clarence, Ralph Richardson as Buckingham

Richard III

Laurence Olivier as Richard, 1955

MICHAEL DENISON

As a schoolboy I was an unquestioning fan of John Gielgud; and as I became more theatrically sophisticated I began to realize why. The voice, of course, the illuminating speed of thought and speech and the glorious talents which surrounded him as planets to his sun, created an unsubsidized National Theatre in Shaftesbury Avenue and were the chief glory of my early theatre-going. But my debt to him goes deeper. Quite simply it is because of him that I am an actor and for nearly sixty years now I have never ceased to be grateful.

His responsibility was quite unwitting. In 1936 I played three small parts in an amateur production of *Richard III* at Oxford directed by John and Glen Byam Shaw with designs by Motley and Vivien Leigh playing the Queen. At the beginning of rehearsals I had no intention of becoming a professional actor; by the end of the production I had no intention of being anything else. Thanks to John, I felt I had come home. I had.

I had to wait nearly twenty years for the special experience of being directed by John to be repeated, playing Aguecheek for him at Stratford with Laurence Olivier as Malvolio and Vivien as Viola.

Suitably awe-struck I decided to read the play as though I had never read it before or seen it performed. This of course proved impossible, particularly as all the Aguecheeks I had seen had bounced on in a very jolly manner, when it is obvious from the text that the poor fellow is depressed. After all, he has spent a fortune and got nowhere in his courtship of Olivia and has decided to go home. I was rather proud of what I thought of as my discovery and longed to reveal it at rehearsal.

'Now you know what the set looks like, Michael?' said John when the great day came. 'Yes, John.'

'Well I want you to appear up left, see Toby and Maria over the little low hedge, wave to them cheerfully – "Woo-Woo!" – then disappear behind the summer house, and when you reappear go "Woo-Woo!" again and join them.' I was aghast.

'Yes, I see, John,' I said with desperate politeness. 'The only thing is, it seems to me that he should be sad. After all . . .'

'Sad?! Sad? No. Terribly gay. Terribly gay.'

So I loyally and self-consciously went 'Woo-Woo'.

When my scene was over I went and sat on the steps in the rehearsal room and was suddenly aware that I was sharing a tread with Larry.

'You're perfectly right, you know,' he whispered. 'Would you like me to try and do something about it?'

'I would,' I replied.

'Leave it to me,' he said as lunch was called and he and Vivien and John went off together.

Sharp at two they were back.

'Michael, Michael, where are you?' cried John, bubbling with enthusiasm.

'Here, John.'

'Larry's had a marvellous idea – that you should be sad at the beginning of that scene.'

I was just about to claim paternity for the idea when I saw Larry's warning look over John's shoulder.

'Oh yes. That'll be a great help. Thank you, John.'

'Don't thank me, thank Larry,' said John with Olympian modesty. And thank Larry discreetly I did.

I thank John for his long lifetime of service to the theatre and for showing me the way into his world all those years ago.

JOHN MOFFATT

Two stories about Gielgud's production of *Twelfth Night* at Stratford (Olivier as Malvolio; Vivien Leigh as Viola): after endless chopping and changing through rehearsals JG rang LO in the small hours of the morning and said, 'Larry, I've had an idea. I think you should play Malvolio very very fat.' Larry, who had been awakened from a deep sleep, said, 'John . . . it's 1.30 in the morning!' to which JG replied, 'Oh, all right then . . . very very thin!'

After the final performance JG called the cast together and gave them notes. Vivien Leigh said very politely, 'John . . . everyone knows of the difficulties we've all undergone and, after this, I don't think anyone in the profession will ever want to work with you again,' and JG replied, 'Edith [Evans] might . . . at a pinch.'

Nude With Violin

NOËL COWARD

Thursday 27 September 1956   Dublin

Well, I now know the worst and the best and the in-between about *Nude with Violin* and can act accordingly. Actually I have been the centre of such a carry-on during the last few days that I can hardly see straight, but I can at least see straight enough to realize that the play needs stringent cutting, a bit of rewriting, and a hundred per cent redirecting. John, to my infinite relief, is so very much better than I thought he would be that my real apprehensions are gone. He looks fine and, although not yet comedically sure, is neither embarrassing nor mannered, both of which I dreaded he would be. There are a few Terry ringing tones in his voice but these can be eliminated.

Sunday 13 March 1966

I am *not*, repeat *not*, going to accept Johnny's sweet offer of his house. It has *no* central heating and the bath and loo are on the top floor *above* the main bedroom. It is also terribly *bijou* and I should go mad in it in two days.

From *The Noël Coward Diaries*

Nude With Violin, JG as Sebastien, Globe Theatre, 1956

The Ages of Man

PETER USTINOV

I once saw him on a local late-night television interview in Saint Louis, Missouri. He was busy playing *The Ages of Man*, his one-man show, in half a ball-park, and now he was being interviewed by a long-winded intellectual.

'One final question,' the interviewer said. 'Sir . . . Sir Gielgud . . . did you . . . oh, you must have had . . . we all did . . . at the start of your very wonderful . . . very wonderful and very meaningful . . . let me put it this way . . . did you have someone . . . a man . . . or . . . or indeed, a woman . . . at whom you could now point a finger and say . . . Yes! . . . This person helped me when I . . .'

By now John understood what was being asked of him, and he prepared to answer, disguising his dislike of all that is pretentious by a perfect courtesy.

'Yes, I think there was somebody who taught me a great deal at my dramatic school, and I certainly am grateful to him for his kindness and consideration toward me. His name was Claude Rains.'

And then, as an afterthought, he added – 'I don't know what happened to him. I think he failed, and went to America.'

From *Dear Me*

Ian McKellen remembers learning so much from listening to the recording of The Ages of Man: 'because there is so much to learn from it . . . the rapidity with which he delivers the lines. The agility with which the poet's mind and the character's mind are revealed!'

KENNETH TYNAN

I had expected successes like these from Sir John; what I had forgotten was his narrative virtuosity. To passages that tell a story – Clarence recounting his nightmare, Hotspur describing a brush with a fop on the battlefield, Cassius tempting Brutus with splenetic anecdotes about Caesar – he brings a graphic zeal that is transfixing. Like the spider's touch in Pope's poem, his voice 'feels at each thread, and lives along the line'. The impact of the performance is not, however, exclusively aural; as I've said, Sir John's physical inexpressiveness does not extend above the collar stud. Poker-backed he may be; poker-faced he certainly isn't. Wherever pride, scorn, compassion, and the more cerebral kinds of agony are called for, his features respond promptly, and memorably.

From *A View of the English Stage*

JOYCE GRENFELL

To the Haymarket to see John Gielgud in his *Ages of Man* programme. The beauty of his voice moves me so terribly that I was looking through tears. So was he. I never saw a man cry so much. A lounge suit isn't right for Lear. Better when I closed my eyes. Not that any of that matters. He is a giant, and he does make me see the horses 'printing their proud hoofs i' the receiving earth'.

From *In Pleasant Places*

BEATRICE LILLIE

One day whilst driving through Leeds, Beatrice Lillie saw a marquee advertising The Ages of Man *with John Gielgud:* She ordered John to stop the car and dashed into the stage entrance. The doorman recognized her immediately, but she begged him just to announce that 'Her Ladyship' wished to see Sir John. As she rounded the doorway to Gielgud's dressing-room, he glanced into the mirror, shook his head and smiled as he muttered, 'Oh, it's you! I wasn't sure whether it was Peggy Ashcroft or Noël Coward.'

From *Beatrice Lillie*

The Cherry Orchard

The Cherry Orchard, JG as Gaev, Judi Dench as Anya, Dorothy Tutin as Varya, Aldwych, 1961

CONSTANCE CUMMINGS

When I think of John's performances, the one moment that always comes to my mind first is a small, quiet moment in Act 2 of *The Cherry Orchard* as Gaev stands apart, fingering a small wallet absently, and says to no one in particular, 'I have been offered a job in a bank – 6,000 roubles a year.' You could *hear* him thinking, 'What an absurd idea . . . that trip to town was really useless . . . what should I do in a bank . . . that's not going to save the orchard . . . me in a bank . . . good God . . .'

How did he do it? All he said was, 'I have been offered a job in a bank.'

How did he spin this magic?

Perhaps Prospero can tell us.

GEORG SOLTI

In 1958 I was conducting the Los Angeles Philharmonic. One afternoon I went to a Gielgud Shakespeare recital. The matinée was a milestone in my life. As the great master, without the help of props, scenery or costume, brought to life one after another of the Shakespeare characters, I understood and enjoyed for the first time in my life the beauty of the English language.

When I came to live in England, my first new production at Covent Garden was Britten's *A Midsummer Night's Dream*, directed by John Gielgud. At one of our first rehearsals together I hardly dared to speak – his English was so beautiful and perfect, mine so bad and distorted. One day we were in a small room rehearsing Puck's final monologue. I was at the piano, while Gielgud was instructing the boy playing Puck. Failing to make a particular point, Gielgud said, 'Look, watch me – I'll show you how I want it.' With that this elegant British gentleman, in his immaculate suit and shoes, stepped on to the makeshift platform. Suddenly we heard the voice of a gleeful adolescent and there before us stood the cheeky and glorious boy Puck.

Since that moment I have been John's greatest fan.

The School for Scandal, Geraldine McEwan as Lady Teazle, Haymarket, 1962

The School for Scandal

GERALDINE McEWAN

I was very much in awe of John when I started rehearsing Lady Teazle in his production of *The School for Scandal* [in 1962]. John, Gwen Ffrangcon-Davies and I were going into the cast (Ralph Richardson was already playing Sir Peter) for the last seven weeks at the Haymarket before taking the play to the USA.

At the end of the second day he came up to me and I was sure that I was going to get some serious and detailed criticism. He looked at me with those sparkling eyes, rubbed his hands together and said, 'Oh, I do love acting with you.' I walked out into the Haymarket on cloud nine!

JOHN GIELGUD

I had terrible trouble with Ralph because he wouldn't decide how he was to come on in the first scene, and kept on holding up rehearsals and wasting time.

JG: Come on, Ralph, you must decide. How are you going to come on in the first scene?

RR: Well, you know, Johnny, I prayed to God last night before I went to bed. I said, 'Please God tell me how to come on in the first scene.' And you know, this morning God answered. God told me to do what it says in the book – *just come on.*

Five Finger Exercise

KEITH BAXTER

Gielgud has always been known as a difficult and demanding director who suffered from an over-active brain and an over-creative theatrical intelligence and who changed his mind about everything every day. On this occasion he was at his most querulous and tiresome. 'Oh, Michael, it's so *boring* just to come down a staircase,' he said to Michael Bryant, who was playing the young Austrian tutor, 'I think you ought to come in through the French windows.'

'But, John, how can I come in through the French windows when the audience has just seen me go upstairs to the study?' he protested, not unreasonably. 'Have I climbed down a drainpipe?'

'Oh, Michael, . . . you are so . . . so . . . *dreary* . . .'

From *Binkie Beaumont*

ROLAND CULVER

John Gielgud has the happy knack of getting the best out of his cast, but I should warn any young actor who may be privileged to be directed by him not to mark the stage moves on the script in ink, as at the end of a couple of weeks' rehearsals, each page might well resemble a pattern of tangled knitting, John being a little hazy for some time as to where on the stage the actor should be at any given moment. If you must mark your script, not a practice of mine, use a pencil, have a good large piece of Indiarubber to hand, and by the dress rehearsal you will know exactly where you are. John's method, of course, takes a lot of the monotony out of rehearsals, each day is an adventure and one is kept on one's toes.

From *Not Quite a Gentleman*

J C TREWIN ON JG'S VOICE

A Stradivarius controlled by a master.

Inflections that undulate like a drawing of the South Downs.

A voice that moved forward like the springing into light of a chain of hilltop beacons,
fire answering fire.

Tartuffe, JG as Orgon, Old Vic, 1967

The Charge of
the Light Brigade

The Charge of the Light Brigade, Harry Andrews as Lord Lucan

TONY RICHARDSON

John Gielgud is, quite simply, the nicest, most human actor I've ever worked with. He adores the theatre, theatre gossip, actors, actresses – he is steeped in them – but he equally adores books, poetry, music, films, travel.

What he likes delights him and he can delight you with his delight. And what he loathes he can amuse you with. He is a constant responder, a constant enjoyer. That is what has kept him so perpetually young, and perhaps is why he has outlasted so many of his great contemporaries who have fallen by the wayside.

To work with him for the first time was pure joy, as it always is.

From *Long Distance Runner*

JG as Lord Raglan, David Hemmings as Capt. Nolan, Trevor Howard as Lord Cardigan, 1967

VIVIEN LEIGH

One day Vivien was sunbathing by the pool and Gielgud was in it. Vivien assumed he swam because he would remain in the water for hours at a time. But he actually waded back to the shallow end, making it appear that he was swimming. When Vivien heard a faint cry – 'Help – help –' she looked up. Gielgud had stepped accidentally into the deep end and was flailing about. Down he went. Vivien thought he was clowning and paid no attention. Up he came again. 'Oh, do please help,' he whimpered swallowing water as he gasped the words and sank below the water again. Vivien leaped to her feet, dashed to the edge of the pool and dived in, pulling him from under the water and swimming with him to the edge of the pool. Somehow she managed to push him onto the ledge, whereupon she jumped out and began mouth to mouth resuscitation.

From *Vivien Leigh: A Biography*

MILTON GOLDMAN

Milton Goldman recalls having lunch with his client John Gielgud at the Four Seasons in 1967. That morning's paper carried the story that producer Alexander Cohen had bought the rights to *Madame Sarah*, Cornelia Otis Skinner's biography of Sarah Bernhardt, and was planning to make a musical from it.

'I suppose,' said Sir John with a glint in his eyes, 'Barbra Streisand will play the first two acts, and Dame Judith Anderson take over in the third with a wooden leg.'

From *Broadway Anecdotes*

Oedipus

IRENE WORTH

This is how it happened and now that there are so many variations on the theme I am compelled to tell it again.

John's sense of fun is contagious, his puns in a direct line from Shakespeare and nothing sharpens his wit faster than imminent peril. The moment was approaching, peril was near, tension had mounted as we prepared for the opening night of *Oedipus*, perhaps Peter Brook's most brilliant production. It was at the Old Vic at the beginning of the new Royal National Theatre under its first director, Laurence Olivier.

It was four o'clock in the afternoon, the stage was covered in gold, we were at the moment when Oedipus had destroyed his eyes and Jocasta destroys her womb and her life with a symbolic penetration by the sword. The sharp obelisk reared before me and I was to very slowly subside to the earth behind it in a monstrous *plié*, the tip of the obelisk touching my chin.

'How is it?' called Peter from the stalls.

'I'm afraid it's too short,' called I, tentatively.

'Oh.' Peter laughing. Everybody laughing.

'What can we do about this?' calls Peter.

'Maybe we should raise it. Maybe we should put it on a plinth,' say I.

John and Ronald Pickup emerge from the wings, choked with laughter. John says, 'Plinth Philip or Plinth Charles?'

Peril ends.

Oedipus, Irene Worth as Jocasta

A thrilling instrument that commands the full tonal range of both viola and cello.

KENNETH TYNAN
ON JG'S VOICE

JG as Seneca, Old Vic, 1968

Hamlet, JG directing Richard Burton, Lunt-Fontanne, New York, 1964

Hamlet

JOHN GIELGUD

When I directed Burton in *Hamlet* he told me that the one thing in which I had been able to help him was knowing where the rests were, so that he did not play too long on hysteria and nerves. I tried to make him find a real line for the part. The play is so familiar that the temptation is to play up the 'show' scenes – the closet scene, the nunnery scene, the play scene, the graveyard scene – instead of making it a play with progressions in which the audience does not know what is going to happen next. It was for this reason that I loved acting Hamlet to the troops during the war. Quite unfamiliar with the story, they followed it with breathless interest, wondering what would happen next.

The American cast did not appear to understand very much of what I was trying to do. All they wanted was motivation.

I was attacked after every rehearsal by desperate actors asking 'What is this character *about*?' I fear that, in the end, my ill-tempered reply would be 'It's about being a good feed for Hamlet.'

From *An Actor and His Time*

CLIVE FRANCIS

Richard Burton was once visited backstage by JG, after his performance of Hamlet – a performance JG did not greatly enjoy. They were going to a restaurant for dinner and Burton was desperately trying to hurry his guests along, many of whom were keen on hanging back.

JG became bored and suddenly said: 'Richard, dear, shall I go on ahead or shall I wait until you are better . . . er, I meant to say *ready*?' JG has since confirmed this story as his 'little indiscretion'.

Forty Years On

PATRICK GARLAND

It was the Age of Aquarius, by now a forgotten and faintly abused era. We were touring The Palace Theatre, Manchester, when *Hair!* set Shaftesbury Avenue ablaze, and by the time we arrived in London, a new morality filled the air. One of my favourite spectacles

Forty Years On, JG as The Headmaster, Alan Bennett as Tempest, a junior master, Apollo Theatre, 1968

backstage during the run of *Forty Years On* was to see in the wings of The Apollo Theatre, Sir John Gielgud dressed as the headmaster of Albion House School, wearing gold-rimmed half-glasses, faded green gown and carrying a dilapidated mortar-board, surrounded by the boys in the cast (the youthful Anthony Andrews and George Fenton among them), exactly like a traditional housemaster and his circle of admiring pupils. Except, of course, instead of yarns about the cricket nets or rugby-football field it was:

'What's your star sign, Sir John?' or 'Have you got Pisces in ascendant?' and 'It's going to be a great week for Aries, Sir John'; and it was marvellous to hear John replying, 'Oh, I'm glad to hear that, Freddie, Sagittarians have been having a bad time lately,' and I swear I heard him say to one of them, 'Do you have Saturn in your Aquarius, Merlin, or are you on the cusp?' And the attendant boys would gather round, waiting for their cue, poring over his outstretched palm. 'Big change of career coming up, Sir John,' they would say, or 'Travel difficulties in July' or 'What a long life-line you've got.' It all seems a long time ago now, the companionship, the success, the fun of it all; several of the boys are well into their second marriages and mortgages, all the memories of that imaginary school are remote, but for Sir John, happily, a long life indeed. He remains the headmaster who never changes and has never aged. Ninety years on, getting younger and younger.

Forty Years On was the start of my career in the theatre, and Alan Bennett's as well, and I believe he will agree with me when I say that neither of us, I suspect, recognized how lucky we were with John Gielgud leading the cast. The play was new, original, and needed a lot of structural work, and the three weeks in Manchester were uphill all the way. My spirits sank one Monday night, with a dispiriting audience, when an elderly Welshman sitting in front of me said at the curtain: 'Well, I give that three weeks in the West End.' He was very cheerful as he said it too, almost spritely. It was difficult to focus the first scene of the play, the headmaster's speech to the parents and old boys, which had to be played 'out front', when Sir John, out of a kind of shyness, almost timidity, insisted on playing it to an imaginary bystander (school caretaker perhaps) standing in the prompt corner, stage left. When I tried to persuade him otherwise, he shook his head, and with a smile replied: 'You want me to do all that Peter Brook and Brecht stuff, and I *won't*!'

Michael Elliott, director of The Royal Exchange Company, gave about the best advice to solve the problems of the play, when he said: 'Do *nothing*.' And went on to explain, rightly, as it turned out, that it was a trick of confidence, not of technique, and that everything would be grand, when we got to Brighton, and Sir John could find *his* audience. He was absolutely right, and all of us thrilled as John made his first entrance at the top of the play, and the audience of The Theatre Royal cheered and applauded for minutes on end. The speech, boldly out front, full of nuance and sly comedy, was a triumph. When I congratulated him afterwards in the dressing-room, he said thoughtfully: 'Yes . . . I had the idea I might try and speak the lines directly to the public, and it seemed to do the trick.'

At one stage, before we reached London, there were still difficulties with the second act, where at a point twenty minutes before the end we reached an impasse, which the boys christened 'the last laugh'. Alan Bennett, who is a meticulous re-writer, was hard at work when John proposed he changed the entire scene – a brilliant but esoteric sketch which parodied Saki, Sapper and Dornford Yates – to something in the style of Noël Coward.

'You know, Alan, you could write something terribly clever and funny about young people and drugs, and I could be sitting at the grand piano and Dorothy Reynolds could be looking out of the French windows.'

Alan demurred at the idea: 'Oh, I don't think I could, Sir John – it wouldn't fit into the design of the play, and I don't think I'd be able to write dialogue like Noël Coward.'

'Yes, you could,' came the reply, 'it's terribly easy. Noël does it all the time.'

A year later, packing our school trunks as it were, the play ended, and Sir John was due to move on – to the Festival Theatre at Chichester, where I now live and work, although I never imagined it at the time. He was going to rehearse Caesar in Bernard Shaw's *Caesar and Cleopatra*, directed by Robin Philips. Now I should explain, Robin and I had been young actors together, and were about the same age, late twenties.

'Do you know Robin Philips?' John asked me one afternoon.

'Yes,' I replied, 'I know him very well, he's very nice, you'll like him.'

'I hear he's rather talented.'

'Yes, he's very talented, very well thought of.'

'He's quite young, isn't he?'

'Robin?' I said, 'Oh, yes, Robin's very young. He and I were both young actors at the Bristol Old Vic.'

'Oh, really,' said Sir John, reflecting for a moment. 'He's not so young then.'

LINDSAY ANDERSON

Ages ago, on a visit to Moscow, I was fortunate enough to be able to give Grigori Kozintsev, the director of both *Hamlet* and *Othello* as Russian films, the long-playing album of John Gielgud's Shakespearean recital, *The Ages of Man*. Later I was very surprised to be told by Kozintsev that John had been astonished when he heard of the gift. 'He hates me,' Gielgud had said. Or perhaps it was, 'He doesn't like me', or 'He can't stand me'. Of course all of these were entirely untrue.

I had met John several times, I suppose, but I had always been shy of this hugely talented and famous actor – much too shy to express my admiration or to pay him compliments. In this I was quite wrong. I hadn't realized that John is and always has been so entirely an actor that he craves and needs praise and reassurance. He has always seemed to have a certain hauteur, but this is due more to shyness than to any awareness of superiority. He has in fact the strangest combination of pride and modesty. About his work he is totally unassuming. He loves to gossip and his recollections are detailed, vivid and witty. But when he steps on the stage it is with effortless dignity, as one who enters his natural home.

I suppose we were a bit wary of each other when at last we came to work together, but it didn't last long. I realized quite soon that what John wanted and expected from a director was intelligence and authority. He certainly did not want to be indulged. He surrenders completely – too completely sometimes – to guidance. He is tremendously responsive and generously appreciative. No director could ask for anything better than the gift of his talent, the quickness of his intuition, his infallible sensibility.

He can be wrong, of course, as we all can. John knows that his impeccable speech, his rhetorical skill has sometimes run away with him. And like many outstanding senior actors, he can be intimidating. But I have never known him resentful or unappreciative of just criticism. He cannot take the easy way out; his every performance is intensively considered, thought through, the best he can do. His audience is never short-changed.

John's tendency to commit the significant gaffe is well known. I remember once being invited to meet him at a friendly gathering. He commented disapprovingly on Noël Coward's public strictures on the younger generation of theatricals. 'They can't help being scruffily dressed,' he declared magnanimously. 'Laundry and cleaning are dreadfully expensive nowadays.' I felt distinctly disadvantaged, sitting there down at heel, having just come from rehearsal at the Royal Court. But I did not feel threatened. Perhaps we both share a certain *naïveté*.

I wish we had been able to work together after *Home*, but he has always been playing in something, somewhere. At least, anyway, that wonderful experience banished my fears – and his. And it began a friendship I shall always treasure.

Kenneth Tynan also said
that he found it a shame
that Gielgud had only two
gestures. In response Sir John
wondered how he could
possibly contrive any more
without the use of
his other members.

Home

Home, JG as Harry, Ralph Richardson as Jack, Royal Court, 1970

DAVID STOREY

The beginning of rehearsals for *Home* was like watching two horses galloping along while, perched on a delicately fashioned carriage behind, a driver called out, 'Whoa! Stop!' finally turning to his fellow passenger and saying, wryly, 'Well, we'd better let them have a run . . .' If *The Contractor* [Storey's previous play] had seen the empirical method of directing at its most demanding, *Home* saw it at its most discreet:

'It isn't possible for an actor to sit on a stage without moving, Lindsay, for 25 minutes.'
'Is it 25 minutes?'
'It feels like 25.'
'Move, in that case, if you feel like it, John.'
Until a point had been reached:
'It's strange, but once sitting here, I don't feel I want to move again.'
'Don't, in that case.'

From *At the Royal Court*

GIELGUD AND RICHARDSON

'One reason I so enjoy working with Ralph Richardson,' wrote Gielgud later in *An Actor and His Time* (1979), 'is that we are old friends and we laugh a lot and seem to balance each other's style in a very happy way. It is wonderful to play with somebody who is so absolutely opposed to you in temperament: we are a tremendous contrast in personalities.' [David] Storey found them so inextricably part of one another's style that it was hard to know sometimes if they were conversing with one another, or saying lines from his play. One night during the run [of *Home*] at the Apollo a man in the stalls suffered a heart attack and the commotion was such that the stage curtain was lowered. Unperturbed, almost academic in their interest, the two knights sat on stage discussing the break in performance. 'Was it your cue that was missed, or was it mine?' They seemed unaware of the cause. The dream remained unbroken. They continued with the play.

From *Ralph Richardson: An Actor's Life*

LAURENCE OLIVIER

I've known Ralph Richardson and John Gielgud for many, many years and we've acted together on innumerable occasions, lately more often on the screen. Hollywood would send for us, the three knights, in the hopes that our names would assist the mogul's box-office receipts. I don't know that it ever did, but I suppose it might have done.

You can hear them in their high-rise Californian offices now, can't you? 'What we need is a bit of class . . . get me one of them Limey guys with a handle to his name . . . better still, get me three.' And there we'd be, the threesome: Ralph, John and Larry.

Looking back, I suppose we all took ourselves rather seriously: when we let the humour and the vulnerability creep in, we get much closer to the truth. This was especially true of John Gielgud in his early days. Now that he appears to regard himself with a sense of humour he has become a much finer actor. Once he threw off the finery and took an honest look at himself in the glass, his acting became much richer and more truthful. His performances in *Home* and *No Man's Land*, for instance, showed him at his stunning best. He is a character actor and it is good to see he's got holes in his socks. He has a delicious sense of humour and at last he is letting it grin through. He no longer needs the sticks of five-and-nine make-up and the voice that wooed the world.

John has a dignity, a majesty which suggests that he was born with a crown on his head; on the other hand my persona is that of a man who has plucked the crown up and placed it on himself. I am Bosworth Field and Agincourt; and John is Pomfret Castle.

Today, for me, John has somehow completed the acting circle. He has found his centre, he is a brilliant character actor. The pain behind the glasses in *No Man's Land* was electrifying . . . the bare soul covered with a thin veneer of sophistication. You could see the clouds passing across his face like a day in an English acre. The sun popping out on the odd moment giving a façade of warmth and happiness . . . not a summer sun, a winter sun. That performance created a reality that I've always fought for.

From *On Acting*

Ralph Richardson on first meeting JG at The Old Vic in 1929:
'I was always rather amazed at him [Gielgud] – a kind of brilliant sort of butterfly, while I was a gloomy sort of boy.

'He was brilliant, he shone, he was so handsome and his voice was splendid.'

JOHN MILLS

Sir John Gielgud, not long ago, was questioned by a reporter on the subject of retirement. 'Sir John, you are over seventy, still playing long parts and acting them with your usual brilliance; if, God forbid, at some time in the hopefully long-distant future your memory begins to fail and you find it impossible to remember your lines, I suppose you will be forced reluctantly to retire.'

Sir John regarded the reporter with a slightly incredulous look on his face and replied, 'My dear fellow, there's always the radio!'

From *Up In the Clouds, Gentlemen Please*

Veterans, John Mills as Mr Laurence D'Orsay, Royal Court, 1972

Murder on the Orient Express, JG as Beddoes, 1974

The Tempest

PETER HALL

On Sunday 24 February 1974 at a dress rehearsal of *The Tempest* at the Old Vic, I nearly cut short Sir John Gielgud's distinguished career. It is an image that still haunts my dreams.

At 1.00 in the morning we were trying the trap door so that we could bring up the chess-game scene. To my incredulous eyes, Sir John dropped through the trap, apparently in slow motion. There ensued a long silence. Nobody in the theatre seemed able to move. I ran and looked down the hole. John smiled up amiably at me as he picked himself up from the pile of chess pieces and the entangled limbs of Miranda and Ferdinand who were waiting below to come up. Miraculously no one was hurt. John finished the technical as radiantly good humoured as ever . . .

Peter Hall

MICHAEL FEAST

During the run of Peter Hall's National Theatre production of *The Tempest* at the Old Vic, Sir John, as Prospero, received many warm and responsive standing ovations at the curtain call. The company line-up was spear-headed by John with Denis Quilley weighing in as Caliban on his left and me flying high as Ariel à droite. Once the basic individual and company calls had been taken, John would step forward for his personal extra bows and then rejoin the rest of us, beaming broadly at Denis and me on either side.

One evening the audience had been particularly ecstatic in its response to the show and to our performances and they really exploded as Sir John stepped forward. Shouts of 'Bravo!' and waves of cheers ricocheted off the walls and roof of the Vic and John's face shone and beamed even brighter than usual. As he stepped back after what must have been a full minute of undiminishing uproar, he took my hand and, leaning over to whisper in my ear, said: 'I think that the landlady must be in tonight.'

JULIAN MITCHELL

One of my fondest images of John is him in the garden at Wotton, presiding over bonfires, like Prospero, not drowning but burning his books.

The Tempest, JG as Prospero, Old Vic, 1974

No Man's Land
MICHAEL FEAST

I have a lovely memory from the West End run of *No Man's Land* at Wyndhams Theatre in which the brokers-men double act of Sirs John and Ralph teamed up again (*Home* was the first time) to magnificent effect. The knights kicked the play off with a twenty-minute scene before being rudely interrupted by Terry Rigby and me as the domestic heavies.

Every night, just after beginners had been called, I would turn up the tannoy in my dressing-room and settle down to listen to the two old chums arriving prior to curtain up. The opening dialogue was almost always the same. 'Evening, Johnnie.' 'Hello, Ralphie.' 'Had a good day, old fellow?' 'Splendid, I ran into Peggy (or whoever).' 'How marvellous.' And then off into five minutes of theatrical banter peppered with famous names and salted with deliciously indiscreet asides.

This would continue until the very second before the curtain rose revealing them, John, as Spooner, pouring the first drink of the evening and Ralph, as Hirst, sitting four square in his centre-stage armchair, perfectly poised in character and situation. The initial Pinter pause of the play would unfold as the audience, at first sight of these living legends would break into spontaneous applause. Finally John would say: 'As it is?' to which Ralph would reply: 'Oh absolutely, as it is.'

Meanwhile, back in my dressing-room, I was turning down the tannoy and getting back to discreetly applying the mascara and checking the flies. An actor prepares . . .

RICHARDSON AND GIELGUD

No Man's Land skilfully and impeccably translated the double act of Jack and Harry in *Home* into Hampstead surroundings . . . and went round on virtually the same refulgent circuit, with the two knights now become, as Gielgud put it, like the 'brokers' men in *Cinderella*. People even mix us up and greet us by each other's names, particularly in America where titles often confuse the public.'

Richardson and Gielgud's near-fifty-year-long relationship was as strong and secure as any in the theatre, and their affection for one another – it wouldn't be going too far to call it a deep though platonic love – was based on mutual tolerance of very opposite qualities. At home, and abroad, when on tour, they kept to their own, now perfected and very separate styles. Richardson would visit the zoo or play the occasional game of tennis, otherwise keeping himself to himself; Sir John would sign copies of his numerous books in the bookshops, and dine out glamorously in the places to be seen in with show people, or repair to the local movie house to glut his appetite for sensation (in Toronto, for example, seeing *Murder by Death*).

They would come together to dispense endless bounty to gossip-hungry journalists, in interviews in which reality danced in perfect harmony with the fictions of themselves which they had, over the years, been no less subtle in forming:

SIR RALPH: Shall we live it up now?

SIR JOHN: Certainly.

SIR RALPH: You're looking very well by the way.

SIR JOHN: Thank you.

SIR RALPH: I haven't seen much of you lately.

SIR JOHN: We meet in costume.

SIR RALPH: We meet as other people.

Then they would depart to their separate waiting cars or Cadillacs – the latter 'usually about that size', said Richardson one night in New York surveying a lengthy specimen parked outside. 'Or longer.'

From *Ralph Richardson: An Actor's Life*

No Man's Land, Ralph Richardson as Hirst

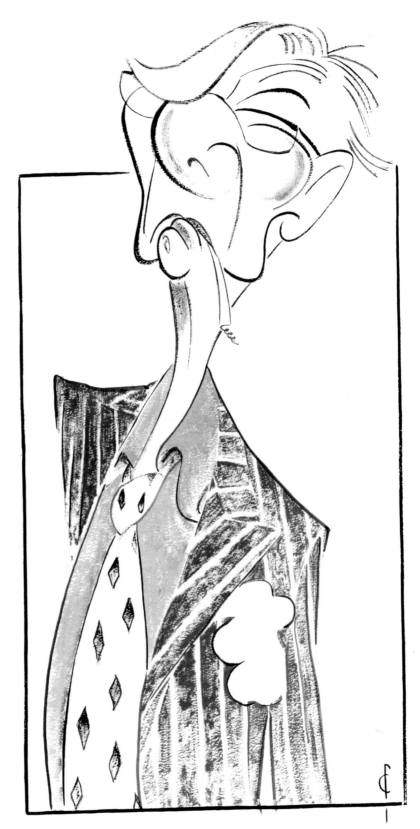

JG as Spooner, Old Vic, 1975

PETER HALL

Tuesday 19 March 1975

A great event. I took Ralph Richardson and John Gielgud for a tour of the South Bank. It was very funny. John, who is nearly seventy, treated Ralph, who is seventy-one, as if he were an extremely aged and endearing relative up from the country, unused to city ways: 'Mind those holes. . . .' 'Don't trip over those wires.' They were both in long coats and large trilbys, Ralph sporting a stick. They could have been nothing but actors. And great ones too. Both sleek with success.

From *Peter Hall's Diaries*

EDWARD BOND

Gielgud played Shakespeare in my play *Bingo*. We had rehearsed in a theatre in St Martin's Lane but for the last rehearsals we moved to the Royal Court Theatre. I watched a run-through earlier in the day before the first public preview. It was in costume and with lights. When they were not on stage the other actors watched from the stalls. Most of them were in their teens or twenties. Gielgud was well into his seventies.

The run-through lasted about five minutes. Gielgud stopped in the middle of a sentence. He said, 'Would you mind if we started again?'

We went back to the beginning. This time the run-through lasted fifteen minutes. Then he said 'No. It's not right. Would you mind if we went back to the beginning?'

He said nothing else and gave no other explanation of why he was troubled. The actors fidgeted in the stalls. I suppose they were anxious to go on stage and get on with their own parts.

We began again. This time more than half an hour passed before he suddenly stood still. 'Would you mind if we started again?'

The other actors shuffled in their seats. There were little sighs and groans. He probably heard them. He said, 'We can't go on if we don't start well.'

The next run-through went on to the end.

He showed no sign of tiredness. There was to be a public performance that evening. He stopped the run-through three times because he knew that if he was not deeply enough involved at the start he would learn nothing as the play went on and so the run-through would be wasted.

For most of the rehearsals – even towards the end – I thought he didn't know his lines. Then I realized that he never made any actual mistakes. He'd been word perfect almost from the beginning. But he always spoke as if he were trying to remember what to say – each thought was rethought each time so that it never became an empty formula. It was only at the very end of rehearsals that the perfect cadences came. They were formed through constant exploring and intense concentration. Most actors decide where the main emphasis of a line lies. He spoke a line as if it had seven or eight main emphases.

Once, after the play had opened, I slipped into the theatre half-way through a performance. As I quietly opened a door at the back of the stalls, an actress spoke a line with extraordinary simplicity and authority. It was absolutely right and seemed to come from a different actress. When I told her how well she had said it, she made a face and said, '*He* told me how to say it.'

During the first night he found himself uncontrollably crying. It was strange. The next day he asked me why it had happened and said it had never happened to him before. I didn't answer.

I remember how he walked when he played Lear in the hovel scene when Lear is mad – lifting his bare feet high and bringing them down gently as if he were treading on egg shells scattered on clouds – like a somnambulistic pelican.

One night I watched him from the side of the stage as he played *Bingo*. I sat on the floor in the cramped prompt corner. To get on and off stage he had to step over my outstretched legs. He did it with his mad Lear walk. I was content and blissfully at peace.

DIRK BOGARDE

Towards the end of work at the château, on June 3rd to be exact, Resnais had a birthday. The troupe decided to club together and get him a tape-recorder because he didn't own one, so we all put our offerings in a hat and someone went off to Lovely Limoges (as it had now become to us all) and bought the best model available. Which wasn't much of a deal. Nevertheless it would be the main offering from a devoted and loving troupe of actors.

There was one small problem. They felt that it was essential that the first voice to be recorded on the virgin tape should be John's. And that he should say, 'This is John Gielgud wishing you a happy birthday, Alain, on behalf of the troupe and actors of "Providence".' Or words to that effect. We all knew that Resnais was passionate about John's voice, indeed he had told me long before that he was determined to immortalize the splendour of the voice and the actor on film; which is what he was doing at the present moment. It seemed ironical that such a signal honour should come from France, and not his own country . . . however: Resnais did so.

The troupe left it to me to ask him to speak these lines on to the tape and dispatched me across the grassy terrace to where he was sitting doing *The Times* crossword. He heard me out politely and refused absolutely.

'But John, why? It's such a little thing.' I could see the troupe standing some way off watching anxiously.

'My dear boy,' he said. '*I'm* not the star of the film. You are. It's *your* job.'

'You *are* the star, for God's sake.'

He looked up with a grin. 'You have top billing. So *you* are.'

I walked back to a saddened troupe. 'He won't.'

Their disappointment was so obvious, so dejected did they look, that I decided to go back and have another try. I knelt beside John's chair in my most supplicatory manner, and spoke to him in a low voice. For the troupe had inched nearer anxiously.

'Now John, listen. They want Alain to hear your voice on the tape; for it to be the first sound recorded on the new machine. Their gift.'

He didn't even look up: shook his head, printed a word, deliberately, in the white spaces of his crossword.

I was desperate. 'John. Please. You probably have one of the most beautiful English-speaking voices in the world . . .'

He looked up over the top of his glasses. 'THE!' he said sharply.

And spoke the message.

From *An Orderly Man*

ANNETTE CROSBIE

About twenty years ago when I was filming *Edward VII* for television, I walked into the rehearsal room one morning in a state of acute nervousness because Sir John was joining us to play Disraeli. He'd been an idol of mine since I'd been aware of actors at all and now, because I was playing Queen Victoria, I was going to act with him.

The director, John Gorrie, introduced us and I said something crass but completely sincere about it being a great honour to work with him, to which he replied: 'Yes, isn't it!'

That's when I realized he was in a worse state of nerves than I was.

Edward VII, JG as Disraeli, Annette Crosbie as Queen Victoria, 1975

I am, I hope, a professional. I try by what I do in the theatre to serve my author; to entertain an audience, arouse their interest, evoke their sympathy, passion, or hatred, to take them out of themselves, to enable them to pass three hours agreeably. If they can be moved, uplifted, amused or fascinated by what they have seen me do, I count myself lucky – though not necessarily successful.

JOHN GIELGUD

JOHN SCHLESINGER

Sir John was a memorable Julius Caesar in a not so memorable production I once directed at the National Theatre. The other leading roles were cast with younger and, in some cases, inexperienced actors.

At rehearsal, 'Et tu Brute' was followed by the throwing down of a raincoat so that Sir John could return to his crossword puzzle.

There came a time when he had to remain on the floor, playing dead. As the scene continued over his prone and very still figure, the atmosphere was thick with memories of his Cassius and Brutus from the past, almost daring the actors playing those parts to speak those same lines. They were nervous.

During the final rehearsal of the forum scene, the bier was carried in with a shroud dummy on it and John would occasionally look up from his crossword, listening to a very Scottish Mark Antony. Something was missing. The dummy always looked like one and so I asked John if he would take its place. 'Oh, I knew you would in the end,' came the reply in his much imitated voice.

I never saw an actor lie so still throughout the final rehearsal and performances. His silence speaks volumes.

Stillness – the ability to listen – is a quality that I shall always remember and add to so many others that this great actor possesses.

John Schlesinger

The Elephant Man

The Elephant Man, JG as Carr Gomm, with Wendy Hiller as Mrs Householders

Anthony Hopkins as Treves and John Hurt as The Elephant Man, 1980

ANTHONY HOPKINS

I was standing in the pub next to the Old Vic in 1968. I had just returned from France having made *The Lion in Winter*. My right arm was embalmed in a huge plaster of paris cast, having broken my wrist and forearm falling off a horse in the last shot of the film. John Gielgud was in the pub having a lunchtime drink with some of the cast of Peter Brooke's *Oedipus* which he was then rehearsing. I was introduced to him and he tapped the plaster of paris cast and said, 'Had an accident?' I went into a lengthy explanation – something like – 'I was sitting on this horse in full armour' (I am not an experienced rider) 'and suddenly, without warning, before I could grab the reins, off he galloped and I fell off, thus breaking my arm.' John Gielgud listened to this explanation – there was a pause – then he said, 'What an old slyboots' – another pause – 'I had to ride a horse in *Becket* with Richard Burton – terrifying experience – could never find the brake.'

WENDY HILLER

The first time that I was directed by John, it was his first too as a director, I was one of thirty-two nuns in that Spanish play, the name of which I can't remember.

At the dress rehearsal, which my husband also attended, we were sitting in the darkness at the back of the stalls. John was walking about in the front stalls, deep in thought. I think we must have all broken out into noisy talk and chatter for he suddenly threw up his hands and called at the top of his voice, 'Be quiet everyone. I'm in a frenzy.'

'Be quiet everyone. I'm in a frenzy' came into the family language. We still shout it when things have got too much for us.

ANNA MASSEY

So much has been written about John's genius, his brilliant wit and mercurial talent but I would like to tell a tale of his unbelievable kindness. I have had the great fortune to have been directed by John and to have acted with him on more than one occasion. A long time ago I was in a play with John and in my private life I was going through a particularly sad and difficult time. I did not speak to him of this naturally, trying to leave my problems at the stage door.

The run ended and three days later the most superb bouquet of flowers arrived with a note, written in his immaculate, tiny handwriting – a note of such gentleness, understanding and compassion that I shall treasure it for ever. He had known of my troubles but his manners and tact are supreme; nothing was mentioned till the time was right. He is the most perfect *gentleman*. I cherish him.

DOROTHY TUTIN

One evening rehearsing *Othello* in the Conference Hall [a rehearsal room in Stratford], Peggy Ashcroft and I arrived early and found John rehearsing with Zeffirelli – the reputation speech. The room was dark and it was raining I remember, we sat quietly and heard the most beautiful rendering of the speech – swift, natural and so moving that when we turned to each other tears were pouring down our cheeks.

ROBERT HARRIS

John, who has always been generous in giving, some time ago came to supper after his play and opened a brown paper parcel revealing a charming oil painting of Camden Lock by Algernon Newton (Robert Newton's father) and asked if I would like to have it. To conceal his generosity he explained that he had so many important paintings he did not know where to hang it!

GLENDA JACKSON

I once met John Gielgud in the foyer of the Beverly Hills Hotel. He was over there doing a pilot for a TV show. Nobody had recognized him and so we invited him to have dinner with us. When he had overcome his initial shyness, he entertained us to a wonderful series of stories.

During the filming of Charlton Heston's *Julius Caesar*, he told us, Heston decided that as marathon athletes had originally been naked when they ran, in the film they should run in naked to the orations. After the naked auditions had been held, he commented 'Buttocks wouldn't melt in their mouths.'

Blackballed for the second time from the Garrick Club, in answer to the question, 'Were there many blackballs?' Gerald du Maurier is reputed to have replied 'Have you ever seen sheep shit?'

MAGGIE SMITH

Since we'd last worked together, he had, of course, been to see the movie *Travels With My Aunt*. One day in rehearsal for *Private Lives*, he interrupted a scene to give me an impulsive note: 'Oh, don't do it like that, Maggie, don't screw your face up. You look like that terrible old woman you played in that dreadful film . . . Oh no, I didn't mean *Travels With My Aunt*.'

Arthur

JOHN GIELGUD

We filmed for a whole week during a terrific heat wave in front of The Plaza Hotel, with cars driving up and down and a queue of people trying to look on, and us sitting in the front looking rather grand. It was also a tremendous baptism of fire, because one had to ignore this large crowd that was watching.

Then, on the second day, one of the pedestrians who was walking by refused to move. The assistant director went to try to move him but to no avail. So the director came over and they got into a fight and were rolling about in the middle of Fifth Avenue. He turned out to be a junkie and had to be taken away by the police.

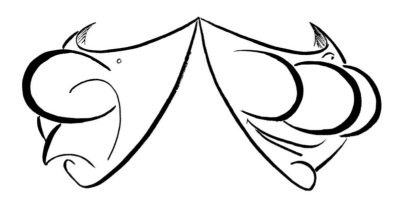

Arthur, Dudley Moore as Arthur

JG as Hobson, 1981

Brideshead Revisited, JG as Edward Ryder, 1983

JUDI DENCH

The New (now the Albery) and Wyndham's Theatres back on to each other across an alley. Sir John was appearing at Wyndham's and saw Daniel Massey at the stage door of the New, where he and I were appearing. He shouted out, 'Hello, Dan. I hear your play's coming off . . . no good?' (Pause) 'Oh, my God, I directed it!' The play was *The Gay Lord Quex*.

We rehearsed for *Quex* in the basement of St James's Church, Piccadilly. One morning, having been rehearsing for about two hours, suddenly, from the gents' loo, a young man rushed out with a pair of trousers in his hand and made a hasty exit, to be followed a few seconds later by another young man *without* his trousers. John laughed so much that we were unable to continue rehearsing and were sent home. We had no idea who the men were.

JOHN GIELGUD

When I was young we wore our best suits to rehearsal and called the leading man 'Sir' – now they wear jeans and call me John.

The Shooting Party JG as Cornelius Cardew, 1985

The Shooting Party

EDWARD FOX

The weather is chillingly cold; the woodland heavy with that particular dank that only the early hours of a February morning in the Home Counties can achieve; the topographical constraints imposed by the terrain on the shuffling lumberings of the film unit are such as render life in all its aspects pretty close to standstill and pregnant with a boredom probably without parallel in the entire history of mankind. Worse still 'the guns', who are about to let fly at thin air and furnished with vast hordes of blank ammunition for doing so are 'actors', for whom blank cartridges and a 12-bore shotgun are generally an excuse for one thing only: namely that arousing from slumber they feel themselves awakened as Born-Again Clint Eastwoods and are about to depict him in some of his most searing moments of drama in a Spaghetti Western. In short, chaos if not actually come, is certainly not far off.

Amid this disarray and awaiting his cue and the word 'action' is Sir John Gielgud, who is playing the part of an eccentric aristocrat of deeply religious conviction and concern for animal welfare. On this particular morning, his role requires that he walk across the line of fire, holding aloft a placard which protests at the activity of the guns and that, whilst the firing proceeds, he walks across its arc at a distance of perhaps twenty paces delivering a long and not uncomplicated speech of protest.

Given such circumstances this task would likely unhorse most of us for the first few takes: the noise, the placard, the rough ground, the speech, the smoke, the cold, the danger, the nerves. For these, or any number of other reasons with which film acting is beset, it would be understood and excused if the actor made a mess of things for one or two goes.

But not so John!

He is word perfect and in need of no rehearsal on that score; has practised earlier and on his own the traverse of his walk; has seen to it that he needs no last-minute adjustments to clothes or make-up so as not to waste valuable time; is standing in for himself, heedless of the cold, still and erect whilst being lit by the lighting cameraman; is smiling, cheerful and calm and ready to pounce onto the required actions of his part at the drop of a leaf.

Action! Bang, Bang, Bang! Wildly swinging shotguns. Dreadful noise and smoke!

Off goes John; and crossing in front of us manages to do everything perfectly, exactly as asked for by the director in one go. Re-crossing to his starting position for take two he passes close by men and I, who am brimming with admiration for the courage, stylishness and glorious professionalism he has just bestowed on this little moment, am moved to say to him, Bravo and how brave and brilliant I thought him. 'Oh,' said John in that flashingly deft style that is his alone, 'how kind of you but really I'm so old now it doesn't matter what happens to me.' And without changing step or slowing down for this remark, on he walks to his first position with purpose in his stride and as if a magnet were slightly leading him from the forehead, to be ready with the minimum of anyone's waiting for him before take two.

He is a great actor. Has been a great actor for many decades. He is as well a great man and a great example to us all; everything that happens for him will always matter to all of us.

Edward Fox

DONALD SINDEN

In 1945 I had been performing with ENSA in Burma and had arrived in Bombay ready to return to the UK when John arrived with his company to perform *Hamlet* and *Blithe Spirit* He was minus a ghost and asked me to take it on. Unfortunately, the wheels of bureaucracy had already begin to grind – my passage had been booked *and could not be cancelled.* However, I was able to attend the rehearsals and saw five performances of *Hamlet* and three of *Blithe Spirit*. I had already seen his Hamlet nine times in London – for me, the definitive interpretation (I have now seen 27 different Hamlets and none can touch his). His Charles Condomine in *Blithe Spirit* was – well – not very good, seriously under-rehearsed and at one performance, John, Irene Browne and Hazel Terry had an uncontrollable fit of the giggles. This earnest young actor was quite shocked.

I spent my days with the company, eating and lying on the beach. Conversation was usually theatrical tittle-tattle: someone told me that as his company boarded the aeroplane in England, John had said, 'If this plane crashes they'll have two minutes' silence at the Ivy!' One evening at dinner I asked a stupid unnecessary question: 'What are the most essential things about acting?' With hardly a pause John replied: 'Feeling and timing,' then with his head erect, his eyes twinkled to the side (a favourite expression of his) as he added, 'I understand it is the same in many walks of life.' I had seen him use the same expression in Hamlet when, facing front he said:

> give me that man
That is not passion's slave, and I will wear him
In my heart's core, ay, in my heart of heart
(a pause: eyes only turn to Horatio)
As I do thee.

John's knowledge of 'social behaviour' and historical detail is amazing. I went with him to see a film of *The Picture of Dorian Gray*; he was horrified and kept muttering (to the consternation of others), 'Oh no! No, no, quite the wrong *material* for a first-class carriage in 1892!' 'That photograph frame is 1920!' And so on for one and a half hours.

At the dress rehearsal of a charity performance, he and Elton John took their calls together down a great flight of stairs. Elton bounded down and John cried, 'No – No – Stately – Stately!'

I think there is nobody that I would rather listen to than John in full flight and one of my greatest delights is receiving his letters written in that minuscule hand. The king among actors. How lucky we are to know him.

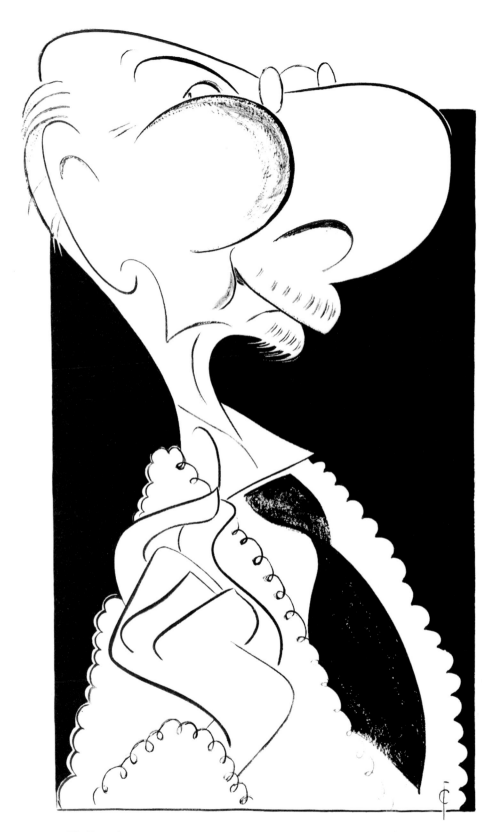

The Best of Friends, JG as Sir Sydney Cockerell, Apollo Theatre, 1988

The Best of Friends

JAMES ROOSE-EVANS

At the age of sixteen, although I had never seen John Gielgud act, I presumed to lecture the sixth form of the Crypt Grammar School in Gloucester on 'The Art of John Gielgud, the Actor', solely on the basis of a small gramophone record of speeches from Shakespeare (which I learned to imitate), and a book by Rosamund Gilder about Gielgud's Hamlet, which described his performance scene by scene. For my lecture I was awarded the cup for Histrionic Speaking!

Shortly after this I went up to London and became a busker, reciting Shakespeare outside theatre queues and outside the Albert Hall, and so earned enough money to go to the theatre. I queued to see a matinée of Rodney Ackland's adaptation of Dostoevsky's *Crime and Punishment* starring Edith Evans and John Gielgud. Afterwards I went round to the stage door (I was only seventeen), and asked to see Mr Gielgud, saying that I was writing a book about him. (I wasn't, but I was desperate to meet my hero.) I was told politely that Mr Gielgud was resting between the shows but that he would be very pleased to read my book when I had finished it.

It was not until some eight years later, when I was already launched as an actor, that I finally met the subject of my lecture, when I was taken by the actor Esmé Percy to lunch with John Gielgud at his house in Cowley Street where he then lived. After that we met many times and after Esmé's death, John would often attend first nights at Hampstead, saying to me, 'How proud Esmé would have been!' But I never imagined that one day I would work with Gielgud, especially once he had retired from the stage. Then, when I was asked to direct Hugh Whitemore's *The Best of Friends*, at our very first casting conference we all said, 'Of course, the actor who should play Sir Sydney Cockerell is John Gielgud, but there is no point sending the script to him, he will never return to the stage. It is ten years since he was on stage last, and he is now eighty-three.' And so the script was sent to one leading actor after another each of whom, unable to see how it would work on stage, turned it down. After three months we appeared to have reached a dead end. 'Let's send it to Gielgud,' said our producer Michael Redington. 'We have nothing to lose.' And so the play was sent off to Laurie Evans, Gielgud's agent, who in turn sent it on to Gielgud who read it and accepted it within thirty-six hours. We were amazed. Michael Redington, who was in America, at once flew back and he and Hugh Whitemore drove down to Buckinghamshire from London, while I drove down from Wales, getting lost on the way. As I arrived, Hugh Whitemore whispered to me, 'He's changed his mind. He isn't going to do it!' I thought he must be joking but Gielgud, entering, said, 'I'll do it on the radio, but I don't really see how it can work on stage, it's too static.' It was at this moment that Michael Redington said to me, 'Jimmie, tell Sir John how you see the play working.'

The play could so easily have been just a conversation piece, with three actors seated in their own areas, and so this was the first challenge I had had to face when I was handed the script. It was only when I realized that it was a play about memory, and that in memory everything is possible, that I cracked it. Once I realized this then the whole text opened up. So, now, I started to describe the play scene by scene, with all its movement and business and sound effects; as I talked so Gielgud began to get more and more excited. When eventually his friend Martin Hensler came in with tea and the dogs, John said, 'Jimmie, tell Martin how you see the play being staged!' When we left, after three hours, it was agreed that he would do the play, but with the stipulation that Hugh Whitemore would make his part larger and insert some more jokes! Hugh and I went off to Stanbrook Abbey and there read the many bound volumes of the correspondence between Cockerell and the Abbess, and it was thus that we found two of the biggest jokes in the play.

Well before rehearsals began John began to learn his part, and I went down with the model, to take him through it, scene by scene. I knew beforehand that he was still nervous about the play and about his returning to the stage, as he had revealed this in a letter to the publisher John Murray, which Jock had shown me. I shall never forget the first day of rehearsal. It is usually my custom to creep up on a play in rehearsal, having done a great deal of research in advance, working through all the technical problems, choosing all the sound, and anticipating the various permutations of moves for the actors. Only then, at first rehearsal, do I throw all this away, and wait to see what evolves from the actors, knowing, however, that if needed I can throw them life-belts in the form of possible moves and business. From the first day we had all the furniture and props, and I began with the first scene, just to get John started. Having blocked it, I suggested we go back on it. 'No, no!' he replied. 'Go on!' And so we went on, scene by scene, until by the end of the first day we had blocked Act I, something I have never done before (and the whole play was blocked by the third day). 'I want to see how it will end!' he said. And when we did get to the end, there was such an evident smile of relief on his face. He both realized that I knew what I was doing and that also the play was going to work theatrically and not be merely a recital of letters. It was quite clear that he needed the reassurance of a framework, the more so in that the play has no plot as such, and so speeches needed anchoring to different activities.

In one sequence the Abbess of Stanbrook Abbey talks about the apple harvest and mentions that she has sent Sir Sydney a hamper of apples. Taking this as a cue, I had Rosemary Harris enter with two baskets and sit at Cockerell's desk, polishing apples and transferring these to the second basket. She then gets up, pulls out a table, covers it with newspaper, and proceeds to pack several crates with apples, each wrapped in lengths of folded newspaper, during one of her own very long speeches, and does this without looking down once, as though she had been packing apples all her life. It was not easy and indeed when I directed the French production in Paris, Edwige Feuillère, who played the Abbess there, used to arrive an hour early each day just to rehearse this scene.

At the start of the scene, however, as the Abbess is polishing apples and talking to Cockerell, I had her pass one to Cockerell, who accepted it with a mock bow. I then suggested to John that he might take a small plate from his sideboard, a knife, and a linen napkin, and proceed to peel the apple in one long unbroken rind during one of his speeches. (I had already tested this privately and knew that it could work.) He at once said, 'Oh, no, I couldn't possibly do that!' And so I left it at that. When he arrived for rehearsal the next day, he said, 'That apple idea. I think I'd like to try it!' And, of course, he made of it as eloquent a piece of business, integrating speech and action, as he did with the eating of scrambled eggs and drinking of champagne in *No Man's Land* during a long speech by Terence Rigby, in no way distracting from the latter but, rather, orchestrating the action with the key points of that speech. Gielgud's handling of props, like his phrasing of text, is a lesson for all actors.

Throughout rehearsals, although he knew the part by heart, he suffered constantly from small blackouts. Each time he would bang his foot very hard in frustration. We were all concerned lest he damage his spine. When Martin Hensler came to see a dress rehearsal I commented on this to him and he replied, 'Oh, at home he always says "Shit!" when he dries, but in front of Rosemary as the Abbess he doesn't like to!' Some days, rehearsals just crawled and we suffered for and with him. Then other days there would be spurts of energy and creativity. He never interfered although one day, early on, he observed that he didn't like being left alone on stage, once Shaw had died, and then the Abbess. Couldn't Ray McAnally (Shaw) and Rosemary Harris (Abbess) just stay on stage, sitting still in their chairs, being dead? I thought it was a daft idea but I did not say so. Let's try it, I suggested. And so we did. At the end he commented, 'No, you are quite right. It's like sitting in a Pharaoh's tomb!' I think deep down he was nervous lest he might not be able to hold the audience alone for ten minutes. The point about the play, in any case, is that it opens with Cockerell alone with his memories and closes in the same way.

Once at the Apollo he was more nervous, yet as the curtain rose for the first preview and the audience burst into applause, he rose to the challenge and seized hold of the opening speech as he had never been able to do before, and delivered it with enormous energy and pace. Once, during the previews, I climbed up into the gods, as I always do, to check if the actors are projecting, and I had to tell him that he couldn't be heard up there. Imagine telling Gielgud that! But he was very grateful. Each preview he polished and honed his performance but was still deeply troubled by the small blackouts. At the seventh preview, the audience included Steve Spielberg, Paul Newman, Joanne Woodward, Tom Stoppard, Edward Fox and Lady St Just. It was on this occasion that he had his worst dry. It came in a speech where Sir Sydney Cockerell describes how he would raise money for the Fitzwilliam Museum of which he was director. The line is: 'I would find a man with no children and a lot of money and get myself invited to dinner; and then over the wine I would say: What are you going to do with your collection when you die?'

At this particular preview Gielgud suddenly said, 'I would find a man with a lot of children and no money. . . .' There was a pause and a slight gasp from the audience, sensing something wrong; then Gielgud corrected himself saying, 'I mean a man with no children and a lot of money!' and he and the audience collapsed laughing! Afterwards I said to him, 'There, you have broken it! So long as you don't worry, the audience isn't going to worry.' I think that night he did overcome this fear, but we gave him his own prompt just in case. However, after that he never needed a prompt and while occasionally there were hesitancies they seemed so much in character with the ninety-year-old Cockerell that no one really guessed.

In his first-night note to me he thanked me for everything, and then added, 'I hope you will continue to correct my faults and be on the look out for any small improvements I hope to make.' Each night he went on perfecting his role, and often at supper would say, 'Did you notice tonight how, by telescoping that line, I got a bigger laugh?' and so on. He always used to arrive very early at the theatre and go to bed to sleep, with a sign on his door saying he was not to be disturbed. And I remember how when I first met him at lunch in Cowley Street, all those years ago, he remarked how he had made it a habit, all his life, to take a siesta each afternoon. He would get undressed, put on his pyjamas, and climb into bed. At the Apollo Theatre after his rest, he would always be on stage for at least half an hour before the curtain rose, in order to settle into the mood of the play. He found each performance a considerable strain and yet each night, at the curtain call, he would look like a boy in love, laughing, years younger, knowing that he'd 'done it again'.

Although in real life Gielgud loves talking and telling stories, on stage he is a great listener. It was the same in rehearsal. His concentration never slackened. He was always totally absorbed in what his fellow actors were saying and doing. Not for him the wandering gaze, the switching off or counting the audience. And this ability, this generosity, contributed so much to the production, to the heart of the play, for it signalled the remarkable quality of Cockerell's friendship. As Cockerell says at the end of the play, 'I declare friendship to be the most precious thing in life. But it is like a plant that withers if it is not beautifully fostered and tended. It is only by constant thought, by visits, by little services, and by abounding sympathy at all times that friends can be kept.'

It had taken everyone by surprise when Gielgud had announced he was coming back to the stage after an absence of ten years and so the theatre was packed at every performance with people of all ages. He gained an especial amusement from the closing lines of the play: 'The Angel of Death seems quite to have forgotten me.' At the age of eighty-three to four the audience was as aware as he was of the irony of this line. Then he would add with a twinkle of amusement, 'On the other hand, I might pop off tomorrow. Who knows?' and begin to hum the melody, 'Tit-willow, tit-willow,' as the curtain fell.

After the last matinée, and before the final performance at the Apollo Theatre, John said to Ray, 'Tonight is the last night,' meaning that he would not return to the stage again: not for him the smaller, cameo roles. He had returned in triumph, and that was enough. The audience that night must have sensed this even though they did not know it for, at the curtain call, as Rosemary Harris and Ray McAnally deliberately stepped away from Gielgud, leaving him alone in the centre of the stage – something they had not done before for, in the nature of the play, they had always shared the curtain call – the entire audience rose to its feet, stalls to circle, circle to upper circle and gallery, cheering, pouring out its gratitude for the greatness and gentleness and wit of this 'most parfait and gentil knight', for his lifetime of work in the theatre.

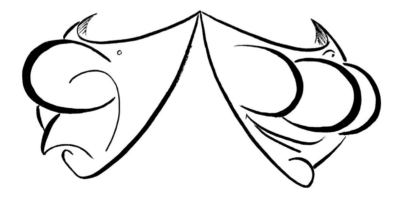

Summer's Lease

Summer's Lease, JG as Haverford Downs, 1990

JOHN MORTIMER

I still can't quite believe my luck in having John Gielgud playing the wicked old journalist Haverford Downs, a character who can't accept the fact that the Swinging Sixties, when he was a sprightly sixty-year-old, have passed away, or that journalism no longer consists of Agate and soda water. My youthful theatre-going was dominated by my admiration for Gielgud and he will always be Hamlet to me, intelligent, sensitive, ironic and princely.

When he turns these precious gifts to comedy, offering an unexpected bit of rudery or screwing in his old literary bloke's monocle as the character admires the retreating Levi jeans of girls in the square in Siena, the result is irresistible.

He seems as elegant and entertaining as ever, his head cocked to catch a whisper of gossip, ready to end his musical sentences in a little burble of laughter at many things, including himself. He comes on to the set in a white jacket, a straw hat and silk cravat, with a perpetual cigarette dangling from his lips, a habit that seems to have seen him through eighty-five phenomenally healthy years.

He arrives in mid-anecdote and within minutes has recounted the story of Marlene Dietrich playing him records of her concerts which consisted solely of applause. He goes on to how Elisabeth Bergner, in *As You Like It*, made Olivier film his scenes with her on his own and then worked out her moves in order to upstage him. He passes rapidly on to Joan Crawford, who, when two admiring dinner guests signed her visitors' book, tore the page out in their presence and threw it into the wastepaper basket with a look of profound contempt.

On another day, on another location (because the houses in our film are amalgamations, the ivy-draped courtyard of one leading into the baroque-painted entrance hall of another), John Gielgud was talking about Lord Alfred Douglas, a beautiful young man who ended up sour and ugly.

'Do you know, Douglas just couldn't tell me. He was Wilde's closest friend and he couldn't remember anything about the production at all.

'Of course, Wilde wanted to sell *The Importance* to Hawtrey, and Hawtrey tried to get the money from the box office of his theatre to pay for it, but they wouldn't let him have it, so then Wilde sold it to George Alexander . . .'

Gielgud's family stretches back through Ellen Terry to the actors of the early nineteenth century; his Polish paternal grandmother was a star in Shakespeare. And yet he's not closed to the future.

He watches *Dynasty* with relish and is reading a book about Lord Lucan. 'Could you really get someone to do a murder for £3,000?' he asked with his perpetual curiosity. 'I suppose Donald Wolfit might almost have paid that to get rid of me. He did' – here comes another small burble of delight – '*hate* me so much.'

JOHN WARNER

Sir John settled himself comfortably, unfolded his *Times* and began to unravel the crossword. David Dodimead, who was sitting next to him, had been working on the same puzzle for some time – but with little result.

After a while Dodimead looked up and was amazed to see that Sir John was skipping through the clues, neatly filling them in at an amazing pace. One particular word caught his eye.

'Excuse me, John, what are Diddybums?'

'No idea,' Sir John beamed back. 'But it does fit awfully well.'

RONALD HARWOOD

Years later, a friend told me of an example of John's absorption in the theatre, which cropped up quite unexpectedly. The two of them, playing in the same film, were sitting on the set in their canvas chairs, whiling away one of the long waits; John was reading. The other, wrestling with his *Times* crossword, leant over, 'Sorry, but is there a character in Shakespeare called the Earl of Westmoreland?'

'Yes,' John answered, without looking up, 'in *Henry IV Part Two*.' Then, to break the bad news, he turned to my friend. 'But it's a very poor part.' And went back to his book.

From *The Ages of Gielgud*

ROBERT LINDSAY

I worked with Sir John Gielgud on a film called *Loser Takes All*, which the Americans retitled *Strike It Rich* because, as Sir John pointed out, the Americans don't like 'loser' in any of their titles. The film was not the greatest success but I look back on it with great fondness because I developed a very warm friendly relationship with Sir John. One scene in particular always comes back to me where we both had long speeches while being tossed about on the worst waters the South of France could throw at us. The light was disappearing and the crew were very tense and anxious to get the shot in. I was concerned that Sir John might understandably have difficulty not only in remembering his lines but in keeping his feet, as the boat was being tossed about quite badly. I managed half a dozen takes; Sir John managed it in one; but he asked if he could re-do it because he might have stressed the wrong word in the middle of the paragraph. Any rumours that Sir John might have difficulty in remembering his lines were soon dispelled!

My most recent meeting with him was at a Royal Gala of *Cyrano de Bergerac* at the Theatre Royal, Haymarket, in December 1992. Sir John had been invited to give the loyal toast; I was in my dressing-room in full Cyrano make up. There was a knock on the door; I answered. Sir John said: 'I'm sorry to bother you, but is Robert here?' I answered rather nasally, 'Sir John. It's me!' And he said, 'Oh, my dear boy, of course. You are him.' A typical actor. He can remember his lines but not a face.

Robert Lindsay as Cyrano de Bergerac, Theatre Royal, 1992

Prospero's Books

Prospero's Books, JG as Prospero, 1991

The *Prospero* film took me to
Amsterdam for two months and
proved a most fascinating experience – a
hugely elaborate and fantastical
version of the play.
I spoke all the parts (including Ariel
and Miranda!) and the whole film was
as if Prospero was writing the play as
it goes along. I had a cloak which
weighed a ton, and had to be naked
in a pool surrounded by nude attendants
of both sexes, ranging from a
tiny tot to older ages.
I'm a great admirer of Peter
Greenaway, but it's not for everyone!

JOHN GIELGUD

MICHAEL HORDERN

John came to see me in my dressing-room after the play (whatever it was) at the National Theatre. I had just been cast as the King in *Lear* to be produced by Jonathan Miller.

JG: So you're going to play King Lear. Good luck.
MH: Yes, I'm pretty scared, have you any quick hint or tip to help me as I know you have played the part on several occasions?
JG: Yes, get a small Cordelia.

But I didn't (she won't mind my saying) and carrying her 'dead' body in the last moments of that gruelling evening was heart-stopping (almost).

Michael Hordern

VANESSA REDGRAVE

I most of all remember Sir John when my husband, Tony [Richardson], was filming *The Loved One* in California. I was cooking lunches for the script conferences and very proud indeed of cooking for Sir John, for my husband, for the producer etc.

Sir John is one of the most polite and friendly people I've ever met who I could listen to for hours on end – if only I got the chance.

I will never forget his delivery of Prospero's last speech at the end of The Old Vic tribute to my father Michael, six months after his death. It meant so much to Rachel and to Corin to hear him speak Prospero's farewell. For me, it was better than a church service or a hundred nice vicars – with all respects to them.

Thank you for everything, Sir John.

RICHARD BRIERS

Only Ken Branagh could have done it! To get Sir John Gielgud to play the old actor in *Swansong*, and to make a half-hour film of it in two and a half days on the stage of the Criterion Theatre, while playing Coriolanus at Chichester at the same time! I was cast as the old prompter. I had worshipped Sir John since my drama school days and now I was to act opposite him.

The whole thing was a trifle unreal. Always the most generous of actors, he made immediate and direct contact with me in performance. The power of his personality and the enjoyment he got out of the role were striking. To hear him speak Hamlet was of course beautiful. After all, his was the greatest of all Hamlets.

During the 'waits', he would entertain us with anecdotes about Irving, Forbes Robertson and Fred Terry with total recall, and would also be bang up-to-date with what was going on in today's theatre. In fact, his enthusiasm for all things theatrical has not dimmed since he built his first toy theatre in 1912.

Sir John is unique. He is not just revered. He is loved.

Swansong, JG as the aged actor, Richard Briers as the prompter, 1993

Sources

Previously published extracts that appear in this book by kind permission of the copyright-holders and publishers are from the following publications (in order of first appearance):

Sheridan Morley, *Sybil Thorndike*, Weidenfeld & Nicolson, 1977; John Gielgud, *Early Stages*, Hodder & Stoughton, 1938; Emlyn Williams, *Emlyn*, The Bodley Head, 1973; Donald Spoto, *Laurence Olivier*, HarperCollins, 1991; Jack Hawkins, *Anything for a Quiet Life*, Hamish Hamilton, 1973; Anthony Quayle, *A Time to Speak*, Barrie & Jenkins, 1990; Alan Dent, *Preludes and Studies*, Macmillan, 1945; Harold Hobson, *Theatre in Britain: A Personal View*, Phaidon Press, 1984; Fabia Drake, *Blind Fortune*, Kimber, 1978; Alec Guinness, *Blessings in Disguise*, Hamish Hamilton, 1985; Peter Hay, *Broadway Anecdotes*, Oxford University Press, 1989; Claire Bloom, *Limelight and After*, Weidenfeld & Nicolson, 1982; Andrew Cruickshank, *Andrew Cruickshank: An Autobiography*, Weidenfeld & Nicolson, 1988; Graham Payn and Sheridan Morley (eds), *The Noël Coward Diaries*, Weidenfeld & Nicolson, 1982; James Roose-Evans (ed), *Joyce Grenfell: Darling Ma*, Hodder & Stoughton, 1988; James Harding, *Emlyn Williams: A Life*, Weidenfeld & Nicolson, 1993; Richard Huggett, *Binkie Beaumont*, Hodder & Stoughton, 1989; Gary Carey, *Marlon Brando: The Only Contender*, Robson Books, 1985; Diana de Rosso, *James Mason: A Personal Biography*, Lennard Publishing, 1989; James Mason, *Before I Forget*, Hamish Hamilton, 1981; John Mills, *Up in the Clouds, Gentlemen Please*, Weidenfeld & Nicolson, 1980; Joyce Grenfell, *In Pleasant Places*, Macmillan London, 1979; Peter Ustinov, *Dear Me*, William Heinemann, 1977; Kenneth Tynan, *A View of the English Stage*, Methuen, 1984; Bruce Laffey, *Beatrice Lillie: The Funniest Woman in the World*, Robson Books, 1990; Roland Culver, *Not Quite a Gentleman*, Kimber, 1979; Tony

Richardson, *Long Distance Runner*, Faber and Faber, 1993; Anne Edwards, *Vivien Leigh: A Biography*, Methuen, 1977; John Gielgud, *An Actor and His Time*, Sidgwick & Jackson, 1979; David Storey, *At the Royal Court: 25 Years of the English Stage Company*, Amber Gate, Amber Lane Press, 1981; Garry O'Connor, *Ralph Richardson: An Actor's Life*, Hodder & Stoughton, 1982; Laurence Olivier, *On Acting*, Weidenfeld & Nicolson, 1986; John Goodwin (ed), *Peter Hall's Diaries*, Hamish Hamilton, 1983; Dirk Bogarde, *An Orderly Man*, Chatto & Windus, 1983; Ronald Harwood, *The Ages of Gielgud: an Actor at Eighty*, Hodder & Stoughton, 1984.